DISCERNING THE

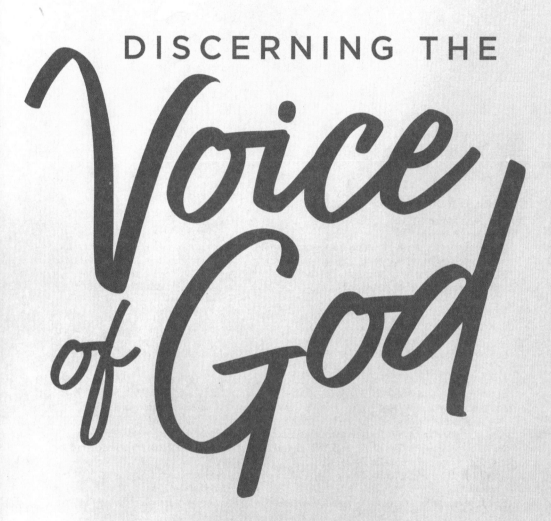

Voice of God

HOW TO RECOGNIZE WHEN GOD SPEAKS

PRISCILLA SHIRER

LifeWay Press® Nashville, Tennessee

Published by LifeWay Press® • ©2017 Priscilla Shirer

Reprinted March 2018

No part of this book may be reproduced or transmitted in any form or by any means, electronic or mechanical, including photocopying and recording, or by any information storage or retrieval system, except as may be expressly permitted in writing by the publisher. Requests for permission should be addressed in writing to LifeWay Press®; One LifeWay Plaza; Nashville, TN 37234-0152.

ISBN 978-1-4627-7404-3
Item 005797596
Dewey decimal classification: 231.7
Subject heading: GOD-WILL \ PROVIDENCE AND GOVERNMENT OF GOD \ CHRISTIAN LIFE

To order additional copies of this resource, write LifeWay Church Resources Customer Service; One LifeWay Plaza; Nashville, TN 37234-0113; Fax orders to 615.251.5933; call toll-free 800.458.2772; email orderentry@lifeway.com; order online at LifeWay.com; or visit the LifeWay Christian Store serving you.

Printed in the United States of America.
Adult Ministry Publishing, LifeWay Church Resources,
One LifeWay Plaza, Nashville, TN 37234-0152

Contents

ABOUT THE AUTHOR

Priscilla Shirer is a wife and a mom first. But put a Bible in her hand and a message in her heart and you'll see why thousands meet God in powerful, personal ways at her conferences and through her Bible studies.

For the past twenty years, Priscilla has been in full-time ministry. She and her husband, Jerry, have founded Going Beyond Ministries and count it as their privilege to serve believers across the entire spectrum of the body of Christ. Priscilla is the author of more than a dozen books and Bible studies on a myriad of topics and biblical characters, including the exodus, the armor of God, Jonah, and Gideon.

Between writing and studying, she spends her days cleaning up after (and trying to satisfy the appetites of) three rapidly growing sons—Jackson, Jerry Jr., and Jude.

INTRODUCTION

Maybe you're like me. When a little window pops up on your computer screen nearly every day—the one that says, "Updates Available"—you always choose the "Remind Me Tomorrow" option. And when tomorrow comes, you delay it again. And again.

Even though installing the newest version promises to make our technological lives better, we ignore it. We're too busy or maybe just too comfortable where we are. But then, over time, our computers start running slower, laboring harder, struggling to perform. The updates didn't seem necessary then, but they sure do now.

Which should make us all wonder: Why wouldn't we want to live *every* day with all the capacity, power, and protection we can get?

Each new morning and in each new season of life, the Father offers us a holy invitation to advance to the next level with Him. Against the common objections of our neglect, disinterest, busyness, and laziness, He invites us to meet with Him, to speak with Him, where His Spirit can speak afresh to us. He comes offering not so much a destination as a journey—a journey into ongoing depths of relationship with Him, a journey into the abundance that old habits are robbing from us—a journey where we'll actually sense His closeness and be led by His Spirit into alignment with His will.

"Remind Me Tomorrow" simply won't do.

That's why, a decade after first penning this study, I'm so looking forward to sharing this spiritual update with you. I believe these insights gleaned from another ten years of accepting His ongoing invitation—not perfectly but at least purposefully—will help remind you what's truly available from Him.

Each week, you'll find four days of insights that culminate in *The Fifth Day*. This is your opportunity to turn your attention inward and really listen to what the Holy Spirit has been teaching you throughout the week, to talk with Him and record what He's showing you. I'm also excited my own father and pastor, Dr. Tony Evans, has agreed to fold his perspectives into each week of your study. In *Digging Deeper with Dad*, you'll find another layer of insight to reinforce what you're learning. A Leader Guide is included as well—just some ideas for you if you're facilitating a group study.

We've got seven whole weeks ahead to enjoy and experience the benefits of what He is eager to instill (and install) in us. So, click yes. And let's go.

A Proactive Stance of Obedience

WEEK ONE

• _obedience_ still matters.

• Stillness is still essential.

• Time spent in God's Word is still the only way to _test_ your mind.

• Faith is still the shield that _____ the flaming missiles of the evil one.

• Jesus is still the only mediator between God and man.

_____ is not only the appropriate response to hearing God, but it is also the _____ that unlocks all the blessings God has for us and opens up the line of _____ between us and Him in the first place.

It's possible to be a _____ leper.

1. It's too _____ to be _____.

_____ is the disguise of the divine.

2. It's too _____ to be _____.

Sometimes the _____ moves of God are wrapped up in the _____ assignments of obedience.

3. It's too _____ to be _____.

Video sessions available for purchase at www.LifeWay.com/DiscerningTheVoiceOfGod.

THE KEY:

TO UNLOCK GOD'S BLESSING

"His leading is only for those who are already committed to do as He may choose. To such it may be said: 'God is able to speak loud enough to make a willing soul hear'."[1]

—LEWIS SPERRY CHAFER

My family has enjoyed a long history with the Dallas Cowboys. I was a very young child when their legendary coach, Tom Landry, asked my father—then a young, 30-year-old preacher—to be the team's first-ever chaplain.

So every now and then as I was growing up, Dad would take me along to some of their football games. I remember walking out onto that vast field at Texas Stadium. From ground level, the turf stretched out in all directions like an enormous green carpet, and the bleachers seemed to extend to the heavens. Mostly, though, I remember Coach Landry. From my diminutive height, he seemed a giant to me—his trademark fedora perched above kind, thoughtful, smiling eyes, exuding a quiet strength. Everyone honored him.

If anyone else personified Cowboys football, it was Roger Staubach, the quarterback who led the 'Boys to two Super Bowl championships in the 1970s. That was a little before my time, of course, but I still remember him and his friendship with Coach Landry. They were both Christians, and they appeared to be almost like father and son. But things weren't always so close between them. Staubach admitted, as a player, he often bristled against submission to his coach's leadership. Despite his respect for Landry's genius in football strategy, Staubach wanted the freedom to call his own plays on the field, to lead the team with his own approach. He thought he knew how best to run the Cowboys offense. *His* way.

Staubach finally came to the point where he realized he needed to decide. Would he rebel against his coach's authority? Or would he get on board with the direction his coach wanted him to go? "I faced up to the issue of obedience," Staubach later said. "Once I learned to obey, there was harmony, fulfillment, and victory."[2] Yes, *lots* of victories.

So there it is. The one word upon which freedom, fulfillment, and victory hinges for all of us.

Will we . . . *Obey*?

FIRST THINGS FIRST

I wrote the first printing of *Discerning the Voice of God* eleven years ago. My kids were only toddlers then and, looking back, I was still pretty wet behind the ears myself. Today my oldest two sons tower over me, both of them nearly six feet tall. Every time I hug them and notice how my head plants firmly against their chests (instead of theirs against mine), I'm reminded how growth is an inevitable indicator of life and health.

The same is true for our spiritual lives. If we're walking with Christ and our spiritual lives are healthy, we should expect to see growth and changes in perspective simply as a natural progression. Just makes sense, doesn't it? And I'm grateful for it—for the renewed perspective God has given me throughout the last ten years or so.

Now, I see clearly that the best way to *begin* a study on hearing God is where I originally *ended* it.

Hearing Him starts with our commitment to humble obedience. We won't do it perfectly—we can't always obey flawlessly—but we must do it purposefully, with ears primed to hear and discern God's voice. One of the surest ways to keep from hearing Him is to adopt a stance of pride and staunch rebellion, in opposition to what His Word and His Spirit are saying to us.

We're not likely to hear *anything* from God until we've abandoned our tug of war with Him, between our wills and His. We may struggle to detect one syllable of divine dialogue, much less receive any clarity in discerning what He means, until we've first opened the floodgates of surrender so He can start piping the volume through.

Drawing a clear connection between obedience and hearing God is a critical piece of discerning God's will and His ways. Prayerfully consider the following verses. After reading each passage, use the space in the margin to record how it connects willing obedience with discerning the voice of God.

"The secret counsel of the Lord is for those who fear him, and he reveals his covenant to them."
PSALM 25:14, CSB

[This is Jesus talking here.] "If anyone wants to do his will, he will know whether the teaching is from God or whether I am speaking on my own."
JOHN 7:17, CSB

[Jesus again.] "The one who has my commands and keeps them is the one who loves me. And the one who loves me will be loved by my Father. I also will love him and will reveal myself to him."
JOHN 14:21, CSB

We'll quell the resounding voice and conviction of God's Spirit within us the more we ignore or disregard it. He will not long waste His words on those who aren't postured to obey. The tender, submissive heart is the one sensitive enough to continually detect God's leading and to pinpoint the strange, alternative voices of the enemy, fear, and ego that seek to lead us astray.

So I've gotta ask you a tough question right here on the first day we're together in these pages: Do you *intend* to obey God, to obey His Word? Do you really *want* to do His will? Or have you already decided to follow your own way despite what God's Spirit will say? Be honest. (He already knows your answer.) I'm challenging you—on Day One—to allow the Lord to soften your heart and to become vigilant in laying down your own ambitions, elevating His will above the pressing nag of your own. It would be such a waste to engage in all these weeks of study together (which I am so, so excited to be doing with you, by the way), if in the end, we keep allowing our stubborn old hearts to stand in the way of hearing from Him.

Please tell me you're not going to do that.

Me either.

I want you to know, I'm well aware of how difficult surrender can often be. Take it from me—a girl with a heart that, apart from the Holy Spirit's indwelling, can be so steely and apathetic. So when I reached out to my Twitter® family, asking them to name the usual suspects that often keep them from surrendering to the Lord, I recognized many of their responses.

See if you recognize any of these scoundrels, these reasons why we don't obey. (Circle the ones that resonate with you personally.)

- fear
- pride
- laziness
- stubbornness
- peer pressure
- procrastination
- lack of trust in God
- uncertainty as to how to begin
- being too comfortable where I am
- impatience with God's timing
- feeling unworthy to be used by God
- being too busy with personal ambitions
- concern that I might be hearing Him wrong
- disappointment in God because of previous experiences
- doubt that obedience will lead to a desirable result

Got any more? Stick 'em here.

Choose one or two of the attributes you circled, and describe how it has specifically kept you from being obedient. If it's not too personal, prepare to share this answer with your group the next time you meet together.

As we dive headfirst into this study and plunge fully into the freedom of hearing the voice of God again (or maybe for the first time), we're leaving these robbers behind. They've distracted and disoriented us long enough. We want to hear God clearly now.

If it seems we're starting this journey at the wrong end of the action plan, putting the obedience cart before the "hearing God" horse, let me just say what I've learned to be true. Facing up to this issue of obedience is the alpha and omega of how we hear from God. Obedience isn't just *one* of the keys. It is *the* key that unlocks all of the blessings God intends for us. It also keeps the door of communication with Him clear and continually open.

No wonder, then, the enemy would want to work overtime to cripple us with fear, stir up our pride, kindle our doubts, encourage our procrastination, or incite any of those other troublemakers against us, anything to keep us from running full throttle toward God in unbridled surrender.

> Look at Jesus' sentiments in John 5:30; see the margin.
> Circle what He did *not* seek; underline what He *did* seek.

Clearly Jesus was not ignoring the fact that He possessed a will of His own. Yet He was committed to honoring His Father's will above it. He heard the voice of the Father more clearly than anyone to ever walk the earth. The defining characteristic of His life was that He was always postured to obey. He was steeped in humility and available to do His Father's bidding over His own sentiments and ambitions as a man.

You and I have our own will too. And that's fine. We don't need to pretend otherwise. Our problem comes from not *surrendering* that will to the Father's superior will. His perfect will. His all-wise will. His all-good will. His "if you only knew what I could do in you, you'd never doubt Me for a moment" will.

Most of us fear the loss of our hopes, dreams, and ambitions should we ever submit ourselves entirely to the Father's will. We imagine them being crushed and discarded, never to be fulfilled. Honoring God's directives will indeed require adjustments on our part, but it will never leave us lacking. The will that is submitted to Him is not extinguished; it is simply surrendered. It becomes like clay in the Potter's

"I can do nothing on my own. I judge only as I hear, and my judgment is just, because I do not seek my own will, but the will of him who sent me."

JOHN 5:30, CSB

hand—pliant and moldable—the raw material for His most stunning masterpieces.

We don't lose. We win.

> In what ways, if any, have you been concerned about "losing yourself" if you surrender completely to God?

Ultimately, submission centers us directly in the will of God and gives us the opportunity to experience the best we could ever imagine.

KEY CHOICE TO MAKE

Surrender. That's the key. Orient yourself toward a posture of obedience—up front!—that's how the door flings open for His voice to be heard and His will to be accomplished. The Lord says to those of His children who freely submit their wills to His:

"I will instruct you and teach you in the way which you should go; I will counsel you with My eye upon you."
PSALM 32:8

So hold it in your hands today. The key, I mean. Right now, in your mind's eye, picture God's guidance and directives to you as a large, ornate, silver key. It runs the full length of your palm, extending beyond your fingertips on one end and beyond your wrist on the other. It's unlike any other key you've ever seen or used before—that's how you know it must be able to unlock something you've never experienced before. It's worth it. This key. It's as unique as your own fingerprints. And it's yours. It is God's specific assignment and calling for you.

Now, right here, right now, at the very start of our Bible study on hearing God, make the commitment to use this key. I promise He will give you opportunity for it throughout this study and in the days beyond. Choose right now, before you do anything else, to receive this key and take seriously the privilege of using it.

The will that is submitted to Him is not extinguished; it is simply surrendered.

God knows what is best and only requires us to obey so that we may experience it.

I know it'll require courage and tenacity. If you choose to squeeze your hand around it, you'll be doing so with a faith that is fully assured of the goodness and timing and wisdom of God. Yet even without full clarity as to what He may ask you to do or where He may instruct you to use it, either now or in the future, make the choice in advance to say "Yes, Lord," sure that this key of obedience will unlock every good and perfect gift your Father intends for you.

Look back at the things you circled earlier—things that are keeping you from surrendering to God in every aspect of your life (p. 11). Offer each of them to Him as you go through this study.

Then, be brave enough to let God search you further. Ask Him to reveal any calloused places that may be blocking you from clearly hearing His voice. Yield to Him any area where you sense resistance and doubt.

You're making a "key" decision here, crucial to being able to experience what walking confidently in His will is all about. Write down anything He's spoken to you through your time of study today.

"Examine me, O LORD, and try me; test my mind and my heart."

PSALM 26:2

THE PLAN:

TO DO GOD'S BIDDING

"I know the Lord is speaking to me when I have an impression during prayer that is consistent with His Word and supported by wise counsel."

—CHRISTINE CAINE

Obedience can be an intimidating word. Depending on our upbringing and other influences from our early life, it may invoke different emotions. For some, it conjures up odious thoughts of harsh, seemingly pointless regimens of rules and regulations that are stifling and oppressive instead of life-giving and fulfilling. For others, it seems oddly devoid of intimacy and relationship, more of a never-good-enough attempt at measuring up. And for even more of us, the word itself feels like a threat to our innate desire for independence. It bristles against the fabric of our self-reliance and autonomy.

> In the paragraph above, underline any perceptions about obedience that you've felt or experienced before.

> What other kinds of defining sentiments do the word *obedience* and its ramifications immediately bring to your mind or bubble up in your emotions?

> What things, people, or life circumstances have been contributing factors to this thought process?

Obedience—at least the kind that our good, loving, sovereign God requires—is neither legalistic nor lacking in affection. Although it places needed boundaries and demands on us—as in, *"If anyone wishes to come after Me, he must deny himself, and take up his cross and follow Me"* **(MATT. 16:24)**—each bit of instruction He gives is born out of the tenderness of His heart toward us and His desire to steer us toward His best for our lives. Obedience is not a *no*; it is actually His best *yes*. It swims in oceans of grace and leads us to freedom, wholeness, and health. It opens us up to His unbridled blessing and abundance.

> Obedience is not a *no*; it is actually His best *yes*.

In the paragraph above, underline any sentiments about obedience that you've seen to be true in your experience.

The irony of obedience is like a delicate dance of trust. It may require real sacrifice from us, while somehow leading to blessing and incomparable abundance.

> "If you know these things, you are blessed if you do them."
>
> JOHN 13:17

- It binds us while concurrently loosing us.

- It holds us tightly while also letting us go.

- It redirects us only to replenish and renew us.

- It restrains us while simultaneously releasing us.

- It limits us while also opening up spacious possibility.

Without our intentional surrender to the former, we cannot experience the benefits of the latter—benefits that are so important and hold so much incredible promise, we can hardly afford to leave them to chance. We must plan and intentionally strategize to pursue them, to pursue obedience. If left to our flesh's tendencies toward rebellion, we will live in a consistent state of resistance toward God and His ways. But if we (literally) *plan to obey*, we put ourselves in position any day of the week to hear what He wants us to do next, and then to have Him bless us with the supernatural joy of following Him.

HOUSE RULES

My three sons and I have a morning routine. Maybe you do too, whether you're wrangling toddlers or teenagers or just trying to get your own self out the door in one piece. For my brood, our morning plan typically involves a strategic engagement of assignments for which each person, or at least somebody, is responsible—bed making, bathroom cleaning, dishwasher emptying, taking out the trash. You get the picture.

Now listen, I'm not saying it comes off without a hitch every day. Don't ask me to take this illustration too far, unless you're willing to come over and help me sort some laundry. And I mean the sweaty, stinky, back-to-back nights of basketball practice variety. The only thing I'm trying to say is, I don't come up with this list of chores on the fly. It's not a random, hope-this-works-out sort of expectation on a busy morning in the Shirer household. That would never work.

Know how I know? Because I've tried that before. And trust me (or say a firm, confident, head-bobbing *amen* with me), it's a recipe for chaos and frustration. It's absolutely essential to work through a plan that's been organized ahead of time if we are to have any hope of success. I need a blueprint that's been prearranged, tried, and adapted through many dangers, toils, and snares. Despite my own affinity for spontaneity and impulsiveness, I learned a long time ago that nothing—and I do mean *nada*—is accomplished during our mornings without a *plan*. Spur of the moment, flying-by-the-seat-of-our-pants operations invite complete mayhem. Only a predetermined commitment to a plan is able (or, again, at least *potentially* able) to hold our mornings together.

Let's pivot here and apply this same logic to something even more important than mama's sanity on an average weekday. Let's talk about that *key* we shared a conversation about yesterday—the key of surrendered obedience that leads to actually hearing from God and being able to live with the pure satisfaction of doing His will. Is anything really more important than that?

No?

Then what's your *plan* for doing it?

We aren't haphazard and arbitrary with a lot of the things we deem important in life: our health, our retirement plan, our monthly calendar of appointments. We even enlist others to help us stay on track with some of those things—help we're sometimes willing to pay for! So, what about our commitment to being spiritually aligned with the God of the universe and with how He wants to direct our hearts? If we don't put an intentional resolve and strategic course of action for following

Him in place, we're basically leaving it up in the air, susceptible to the flighty whims of our circumstances and feelings. There's simply too much eternal treasure at stake for that.

But don't take my word for it. We go to *God's* Word for instruction. In the story of the patriarch Abraham, we find both the value and profitable results of making *plans* to obey. (We'll start considering Abraham's story today and continue it throughout the rest of the week.)

LOOKS LIKE A PLAN

> Read Genesis 22:2-3 in the margin. Look for the following words, then fill in the blanks by writing what the verse says Abraham did in response to God's instruction. ("Saddled <u>his donkey</u>," for example, is the first one.)
>
> Saddled _____
>
> Took _____
>
> Cut _____
>
> Went _____

Old Testament sacrificial rituals were quite laborious. The process was painstakingly detailed and time-consuming, not to mention messy (what with all that slaying and dismembering going on). But in reading a short, concise record of it, like we see here in Genesis 22, appearances can be deceiving. The succinct summary of Abraham's activity in verse three, outside of the emotional torment invoked by verse two, makes the whole thing sound rather easy.

Yet the assignment Yahweh gave to Abraham could not have been accomplished on a whim. No haphazard spontaneity would enable Abraham to follow through on this mission. It was too arduous and meticulous of a task to accomplish without adequate preparation, strategy, intentionality, accountability, and dedication to detail. Each of these would be required in order to fully obey God's directive.

> For each word on the next page, lookup the accompanying verse. Ask the Lord to give you clarity as to how the principles behind these elements might become a more strategic part of your plan of action to be obedient to His will. Jot down anything that really stands out to you.

"[God] said, 'Take your son, your only son Isaac, whom you love, and go to the land of Moriah, and offer him there as a burnt offering on one of the mountains of which I shall tell you.' So Abraham rose early in the morning, saddled his donkey, and took two of his young men with him, and his son Isaac. And he cut the wood for the burnt offering and arose and went to the place of which God had told him."
GENESIS 22:2-3, ESV

Preparation (Neh. 2:7-9,13-15)

Strategy (Eph. 6:11-13)

Accountability (Eccl. 4:11-12)

Intentionality (Col. 3:1-2)

Dedication (Dan. 1:8)

Consider the following as it related to Abraham's plan of obedience.

1. PREPARATION AND STRATEGY: The journey to Mount Moriah in Jerusalem required *three* days (see Gen. 22:4). This meant gathering supplies ahead of time for overnight camping as well as measuring out rations for food and drink, all in order to sustain the entourage as they made their trip to the place of sacrifice.

2. ACCOUNTABILITY: Abraham's choice to bring two servants along may have been to provide help in carrying enough wood to build an altar. But, perhaps he brought them along for companionship as he carried out this difficult assignment.

3. INTENTIONALITY AND DEDICATION: Along with the wood, "glowing pieces of charcoal or other embers would have been carried in small pottery containers and carefully nursed along until a fire was needed."[3]

In each of the previous facts, what do you observe about Abraham's commitment to intentionality in his obedience?

1.

2.

3.

See how he refused to leave anything to chance? He didn't just *hope* to carry out God's instructions. He put measures in place to be certain of it—certain he would arrive at his destination, certain he'd be equipped with appropriate supplies to carry out the task, certain of having suitable accountability in place to make sure the job was done with precision. Every step along the way, Abraham's plan put him in position to hear what God would say or do next.

Now this may not be what we prefer our obedience to *feel* like. But this is what obedience *looks* like. This is what obedience *does*. When Abraham lived out his trust in God by making plans to obey what he'd been told, his faith was rewarded with the miraculous appearance of a substitutionary animal and the subsequent salvation of his son Isaac.

So what about you? What about me?

Will we, like Abraham, prepare to be obedient to God?

- Will we commit to align our actions and attitudes with the direction of obedience?

- Will we take the necessary precautions to cut out people or pastimes that influence us toward disobedience?

- Will we fortify our resolve by intentionally surrounding ourselves with influences that encourage us toward godliness?

- Will we humble ourselves to remain accountable to other mature believers who have our best interests at heart?

- Will we commit to shifting our attitudes or actions the moment we realize they are out of alignment with God's will?

- If you say "Yes, I will," what kinds of plans would help you turn these noble desires into real resolutions? Especially in areas of your life where obedience is the most difficult?

Our answers to these questions will determine the extent to which our spiritual ears are primed to hear God.

If you haven't already, on the inside of the front or back cover of this book, make a list of personal circumstances troubling you. As you work through this Bible study, focus on these circumstances and how God is speaking to you concerning them.

God will undoubtedly be giving you new directives and insights as we journey together through these pages. The question is: What can you do today to strategize a lifestyle of obedience? So when He speaks, you're there—with plans to obey?

Here's one suggestion: If you're doing this study within the context of a group, take full advantage of the relationships you'll develop within this community. See every person as a partner in your journey of spiritual growth and you for them. Each of them has been divinely chosen by the Lord to walk this road with you, at least for the weeks you're sharing this study. Be intentional and strategic about your commitment to obedience *together*. There is strength in numbers!

THE COST:

TO RECEIVE GOD'S BEST

"Our spiritual ear will never be sensitive to his voice if we have a personal agenda to which we are already committed. God leads and speaks to the humble who have surrendered their plans and want to do His will. With an 'open heaven' and a surrendered will, we will be able to clearly hear God's voice in our hearts."

—JIM CYMBALA

My son Jude was only three years old the day I saw him walking around our backyard with his hand stuck in a mason jar.

I'd been nearby reading, looking up every now and then to check on his well-being while he played with his toys. But the sound of his whimpering piqued my attention, and the sight of this new development made me too curious not to investigate.

"Come here, honey, what's the matter?" Drawing closer, he told me in broken toddler language what I already knew: he couldn't get his hand out of the jar. But the best I could tell, the only reason he couldn't was because he had his hand balled up into a tight fist. "Just open up your hand, and it'll come right out."

Ah, but there was the problem—inside that grubby fist was an acorn he'd seen at the bottom of the jar—a treasure he didn't want to let go of. No matter how reasonably I tried to explain that he could get both his hand *and* the acorn out if he'd only listen to me, he refused to release his grasp. He spent the rest of his playtime that day wandering around the yard, still wearing that jar on the end of his arm.

How much fun could that be?

But, who of us hasn't done the same thing? We're all prone at times to hold on too tightly to our own ambitions, relationships, expectations, and even our successes, long after God has instructed us to let them go. In the moment, letting go doesn't make sense. Releasing them doesn't seem worth the alternative. We insist on carrying them around for awhile—maybe for a lifetime—no matter how they may limit or short-circuit the benefits we could otherwise enjoy.

But hearing from God and enjoying the freedom that comes from doing what He says often requires us to empty our hands, trusting He will fill them with something better. And if we haven't prearranged our allegiance, if we haven't preplanned our strategy, if we haven't enlisted suitable accountability—all in a determined commitment to obedience—our wayward emotions will betray us into clinging to things out of rebellion and personal comfort, out of fear and insecurity. We'll miss living in the *"spacious place"* God desires for us **(2 SAM. 22:20, CSB)**.

We must be willing to pay the *cost* that leads to His best.

> Is there an area of your life in which you are currently resisting obedience because of the cost involved in "letting go"? List the perceived cost below.

LETTING GO

Yesterday, we looked at the planning required for Abraham to obey God's instructions. Read Genesis 22:2-3 again today:

> "[God] said, 'Take your son, your only son Isaac, whom you love, and go to the land of Moriah, and offer him there as a burnt offering on one of the mountains of which I shall tell you.' So Abraham rose early in the morning, saddled his donkey, and took two of his young men with him, and his son Isaac. And he cut the wood for the burnt offering and arose and went to the place of which God had told him."
> **GENESIS 22:2-3, ESV**

Talk about "letting go"! Consider the emotionally traumatic toll that God's directive placed on Abraham. We ain't talking acorns here. By any standard, God's instruction was *brutal*—a gut punch to the tender heart of a loving father—not to mention a seeming contradiction to Yahweh's own promises.

I'm sure you've read and heard enough of this story to be familiar with all the irrationalities implied in what God was saying. He had promised Abraham a great nation from Abraham's offspring. And now it seemed He was asking Abraham not only to sacrifice this son he loved but also the future God had promised. A new nation? Descendants as numerous as the stars in the sky? Sort of impossible without Isaac, right? And yet Abraham had clearly heard what seemed an unreasonable, unimaginable command from God: *Let go!*

What does a person *do* with that? With an unthinkable assignment? No one would have faulted Abraham for running away from it. The cost of obedience seemed unreasonably high. While we're familiar, of course, with Abraham's story, we know our own stories even better, which leads me to ask you (as I ask myself):

> How has your response to God, regarding whatever He's asking you to release, been similar or different from Abraham's reaction at the beginning of verse 3?

Perhaps one reason Abraham could do the unthinkable here was because costly obedience wasn't new to him. This concept of "letting go" had become an ongoing experience in His relationship with the Lord. Consider his track record:

> Turn to Genesis 12:1-3, and answer the following questions.
> 1. What was Yahweh's instruction?

> 2. What would Abraham need to "let go of" in order to obey?

3. If Abraham submitted to God's directive, what was the promised outcome?

Seriously, almost from the first time we meet Abraham to the very end, everything God required from him seemed to necessitate a radical level of expense—his home, his family, his heritage, his comfort. Yet, Abraham was willing to pay it. Situations in which he could have easily answered with a vehement *no*, instead he responded with a valiant *yes*. His stance was sure. His compass had been set to march toward God's purposes. *No matter the cost.* He might not have been crazy about what God was telling him. But one thing's for sure—

He was hearing from God.

Because he didn't let the cost frighten him into disobedience, Abraham received the outlandish benefits of God's grace—not only astounding, personal miracles but also a firm foundation for the beginning of a new nation founded firmly on trust and faith in Yahweh as *Jehovah Jireh, "The Lord Will Provide"* **(GEN 22:14)**.

RISK AND REWARD

So Abraham's costly obedience resulted in abundant blessings, not only those that buoyed him and his family for years to come but also those that extend to you and me even all these millennia later. Among the clearest takeaways is a lesson that each of us wanting to hear from God must learn.

Expect to pay a price.

Only an errant, misguided theology would present bouquets completely devoid of thorns. Because, listen, there is sacrifice involved in your commitment to God. And yet from age to age, from one faithful follower to another, from testimonies that pile up behind us into mountains of indisputable evidence—the benefits far outweigh the costs. Believing this truth is essential.

"For I consider that the sufferings of this present time are not worthy to be compared with the glory that is to be revealed to us."
ROMANS 8:18

When we refuse to follow God's direction, it's usually because we're convinced that whatever He's asking us to give up is greater than what we'll gain.

By obeying, we'll see some of these benefits in a physical, visible, tangible way on earth, while other blessings will be reserved for us as treasures and rewards of heaven. But no matter here or there, then or now, God's benefits and blessings will always be far more valuable than whatever it is we feel so resistant to release. Ask Abraham and many others—or simply ask yourself.

Name some clear blessings you can trace back to a decision you made to obey, even when it seemed costly at the time.

In disobedience, we miss God's blessings, invite His necessary discipline, and break the intimacy that allows our spiritual ears to hear what He is saying to us.

If only we'd understand the advantage we're gaining in the exchange.

Look up at least two of the following examples, and outline the cost of obedience to each individual.

Esther (Esth. 4:14-17)

The Disciples (Luke 18:28-30)

Paul (Phil. 3:4-11)

Jesus (Phil. 2:8-10)

We all have to lay something down in order to receive God's best. And when we do—like Paul, we come to know Christ *"and the power of his resurrection,"* even as we *"share his sufferings, becoming like him in his death"* **(PHIL. 3:10, ESV).**

Like Esther, we eventually come to know days of *"light and gladness and joy and honor"* **(ESTH. 8:16).**

Like Jesus' disciples, we come to experience Jesus' promise to them: *"Truly I say to you, there is no one who has left house or wife or brothers or parents or children, for the sake of the kingdom of God, who will not receive many times as much at this time and in the age to come, eternal life"* **(LUKE 18:29-30).**

> As you have launched into this study, what modifications do you already suspect you'll need to make in the following areas in order to be obedient to God's directives?
>
> Ambitions:
>
> Beliefs:
>
> Expectations:
>
> Relationships:
>
> Traditions:
>
> Other:
>
> Which of these would you consider to be the greatest costs to you? Costs that at one time you might not have been willing to pay?

THE TIME:

TO RESPOND TO GOD'S VOICE

Have you ever met someone whose relationship with God is so full, robust, and real that his or her life seems more like a spreading wildfire than a quietly contained religion? *I have.* Through the years, I've crossed paths with many people whose passion for God and their continued optimism about life with Him have stirred my soul.

They fascinate me, these individuals who are radically unique even among other Christians I know. There's just something deeper and more substantial about their walks than the rest of ours. They have a firm, unshakable resolve in God, and their experiences with Him are as mind-boggling as they are flat-out beautiful.

Whenever I meet people like this—those whose spiritual fires ignite my own—I always take time to ask them what they'd pinpoint as the main reason behind their ongoing fervor. And without fail, their answers are remarkably similar. (It always makes me wonder: if the secret is really so evident, why aren't we all doing the same thing?) Here's the repeated theme: *their walks with God aren't centered primarily on knowledge; they hinge on a relationship experience.* These people are dedicated to studying the Bible, yes, but they're also dedicated to aligning their lifestyle with it. The knowledge they acquire from delving deeply into Scripture only whets their appetites for knowing its Author more intimately and for seeing Him at work amid the regular rhythms of their everyday living.

In response to my question, one person made a statement that sums up everything I've ever heard anyone say on this subject. "I decided a long time ago," she said, "the only appropriate response to God is my complete and immediate obedience. I am committed to obeying His leading no matter how absurd, difficult, or unpopular His directive may seem. If He said it, I'm doing it. Immediately."

You want to hear God's voice? Really? Let this woman's answer become the beat of your own heart. Because this—*this*—is what separates the passionate and fervent from the critical and skeptical. This is what separates those who know *about* God from those who actually experience Him, encounter Him, and hear His voice. When the Spirit leads, they heed and follow.

Immediate obedience creates the needed margin for God to invade our everyday lives, to stir up supernatural activity, to cause our hearts to pound with anticipation, and to ruin us for "church" as usual. Seeing God, hearing His voice, sensing His presence near us, and watching Him working through us will make our obedience worth it.

IMMEDIACY

Let's turn our attention back to Abraham. He seemed to understand not merely the blessing of obedience but of *immediate* obedience. He knew the importance of responding to God without delay. He knew there were blessings to be found in a lifestyle of righteous, and right now, obedience.

When the Lord told Abraham to leave his homeland, giving him no further information on where he was to go, he obeyed immediately with nothing more than God's word for security (Heb. 11:8). On another occasion, when God instructed him to circumcise every male in his household, Abraham did it the very same day (Gen. 17:10-14,22-23).

Now Abraham wasn't perfect, okay? The Bible is honest enough to reveal some of his bobbles in character, many of which were quite serious. In fact, Genesis 15:6 says Abraham's *"righteousness"* came from the same place ours does: *"He believed in the Lord."* (You may remember reading about this in the New Testament—Paul often references Abraham's faith story in his New Testament letters.) Abraham was faithful, not flawless.

But, Abraham was good at being immediately obedient. He consistently did what God said, and he did it without delay.

> In the passage we've been studying this week (Gen. 22:2-3), how did Abraham follow a pattern of immediate obedience?

The only appropriate answer when we hear God speaking is, "Yes, Lord."

"If you love Me, you will keep My commandments."
JOHN 14:15

"Abraham rose early in the morning..."
GENESIS 22:3, ESV

What do Abraham's actions tell us about:
1. His internal posture of obedience toward God

2. His readiness to make quick adjustments

3. His lack of concern for conflicting opinions

Put yourself in Abraham's shoes, how might your response have been different from Abraham's especially given the weight of God's instructions?

Would the ram have been caught in the bush if Abraham had delayed his obedience? No one can know for sure. But consider the perfectly-timed intersection of the ram and Abraham on top of that mountain.

When the Lord gives me instructions that I don't particularly like, sometimes to the point that I'm afraid to carry them out, the last thing I want to do is get up "early in the morning" to start putting them into action. It's usually easier to do anything other than what God has said to do. Instead I'll often—oh—think about it, pray about it, or talk to my husband and friends about it. Sometimes I'll even try to ignore it. I can think of times, for example, when the Holy Spirit has convicted me to get up and leave right in the middle of a movie or to back away from a conversation that's becoming unhealthy. He's nudged me to close the cover on a book that, while intriguing, well-written, and perhaps even recommended to me as a couldn't-put-it-down page-turner, is starting to show signs of taking me places I don't have any business going. Yet far too frequently, my obedience is not as quick as it should be. What about yours?

Abraham didn't wait a couple of days or weeks to make sure God was certain about what He wanted him to do. He gave the Lord instant, unquestioning obedience, despite being given some unbelievably difficult instructions.

Has the Lord given you instructions this week that you've been slow to respond to Him about? If so, what were those instructions?

What was the reason for your delay? What talked you out of acting on it? What kinds of rebuttals have you been listening to and leaning on?

Delayed obedience is disobedience.

And disobedience always yields consequences.

We find another illustration of this truth in Numbers 13–14: the record of an event in Yahweh's relationship with Abraham's descendants (the children of Israel). After being freed from Pharaoh's rule, the Hebrews wandered the sandy, desolate landscape of the Sinai Peninsula. Finally, God instructed them to send spies into the promised land to survey the territory that He planned to give them.

Let's be clear on their mission here. They weren't being sent out to determine whether or not the people should take the land. This was more of a scouting trip, a preview of coming attractions concerning what God had already promised them. And yet the sight of the land's inhabitants and the potential problems in trying to occupy it sparked fear in the hearts of the spies, fear that spread like wildfire throughout the rest of the nation. Except for two strong, faith-filled men—Joshua and Caleb—the rest of God's people determined they should *not* do what God had told them to do, *not* claim what He had given them to claim. In fact, they were so frightened that they even wanted to return to Egypt (Num. 14:1-4).

God's anger was kindled against His beloved people because they refused to trust Him despite all He had accomplished on their behalf. God's anger opened their eyes to the consequences of not obeying Him. By not responding with immediate obedience, they cost themselves the opportunity to take the land right away.

Read the people's action and God's response in Numbers 14:39-45. Record your observations.

Is there any way that Israel's actions mirror your own actions right now?

How can you proactively shift your response toward God in this area of your life, so that you're obeying Him immediately?

DELAY

I'm riveted by Paul's explanation of the armor of God in Ephesians 6. This passage has not only given me insight into the defenses at my disposal to help me stand firm, but it has also shined a spotlight on the tactics our common enemy uses to keep me (and all of us) from experiencing victory.

Turn to Ephesians 6:14, and identify the second piece of armor listed there.

How would you define the spiritual virtue that correlates with this piece of armor?

If *righteousness*—right living—provides a defensive mechanism against a full frontal demonic attack (and it does), your enemy's goal will always be to steer you toward *wrong living* (and he will). He'll employ any enticements he can lay in your path to persuade you toward disobedience and rebellion. He wants you exposed, your breastplate unused, your life laid bare and available to every threat and deadly scheme he's planned.

And if he can't get you to *disobey*, he will at least try convincing you to *delay*. The enemy knows that when we as believers align our lives to God through immediate obedience we have a clear means of defense against him—our breastplate of righteousness. And since this piece of armor will always prove too strong for Satan to infiltrate, he conspires to keep it lying at our feet, left at home, or off for the weekend, anything to keep it out of place as long as possible—hours, days, weeks, months, years, *a lifetime*.

Go back to the first lesson this week, and look at the things you circled on page 11 that have kept you from obeying God in the past. Write several of the most frequent ones below.

Delayed obedience is disobedience and leaves us exposed to the enemy's advances.

How can you clearly detect when the enemy may be scheming against you, perhaps using this particular device to delay your obedience?

If the enemy can't get you to *disobey*, he will at least try convincing you to *delay*.

I'm not saying the enemy is the only reason behind things we may be struggling with. (He isn't always. Sometimes it's just us.) But, when I suspect he may be the source of it, I don't know about you, but it causes a holy indignation to rise up inside me. It makes me want to stand firm and no longer allow him to snatch God's best away from me. Sometimes he doesn't even have to snatch it—I just hand it over.

Well, no more.

Breastplate is on. Resolve is firm.

I will honor God's Word immediately, refusing to let procrastination keep me from being able to deflect the attacks of the enemy. I want to receive all the benefits that come to a person whose life honors God.

Let's make this commitment together, okay?

THE FIFTH DAY

"Almighty God, in this hour of quiet I seek communion with you. I want to turn away from the worry and fever of today's work, from the world's jarring noises, from the praise and blame of other people, from the confused thoughts and fantasies of my own heart, and instead seek the quietness of your presence."[4]

—JOHN BAILLIE

I have an ongoing prayer request that frequently peppers my conversations with God. No matter the specific details I'm verbalizing, I always seem to land here:

"Lord, reveal Yourself to me."

The definition of the original Greek word for reveal *in John 14:21 (CSB) means "to exhibit, to appear in person, to declare."*[5]

More than anything else that might define or characterize my circumstances, I want to hear His voice, detect His fingerprints in my life, and see Him moving within it all. No matter how many times I make this appeal to Him in prayer, and no matter how many different combinations of words I use, God's response is always an echo of this verse:

"The person who has My commands and keeps them is the one who [really] loves Me; and whoever [really] loves Me will be loved by My Father, and I [too] will love him and will show (reveal, manifest) Myself to him. [I will let Myself be clearly seen by him and make Myself real to him.]"
JOHN 14:21, AMPCE

In other words, He says to me, *Priscilla, you really want to see Me? Then get busy being radically obedient to Me.* His Word tells us to plan on it. On obeying. Whatever it may seem to cost. And not to wait another second before we start. As backward as it may seem at first, what we do in preparation *before* we hear from God is just as important as how we choose to respond to God *after* we hear from Him. God doesn't just speak to be heard; He speaks to be obeyed.

So today—on this Fifth Day—I'm not giving you anything to lookup. I'm only asking you to *look up*. At Him. Use this time of seeking Him (and seeking to hear Him) as an opportunity to commit yourself to up-front, proactive obedience—before He even says a word.

Flip back through this first week of study, looking for things you've highlighted, starred, or underlined. Read some of the answers you've given to the questions I've asked. Perhaps reread some of the Scriptures you studied that you wanted to spend more time with. Generally, just reflect on what you heard God saying through His Word and His Spirit—into *your* spirit—that left a particular mark.

Then, rest with Him a while. Marinate in what He's been leading you to consider and act on. And as you interact with Him in prayer on this less structured Fifth Day, do what you most like to do when you want to be sure you remember something important. Journal it. Type it up. Draw a picture of it. Write a song or poem about it.

This is your day to listen. When you get up from here, it's time to obey what He's showing you to do.

_____

_____

_____

_____

_____

_____

_____

_____

_____

_____

_____

_____

_____

OBEDIENCE DETECTED

by Dr. Tony Evans

At our church in Dallas, we've installed motion detector lighting to cut down on the amount of electricity wasted when lights are left on for no reason. Now, when someone walks into a room, the lights come on; when the person or group walks out, the lights turn off.

Even so with our God. Just as motion within our church building causes the presence and power of light to manifest itself, obedience activates God's presence and power in our everyday lives. He stands ready to reveal greater illumination of His will to anyone from whom He detects obedient motion.

Jesus made clear the direct relationship between obedience to God and communication with God when He said, *"If anyone loves Me, he will keep My word; and My Father will love him, and We will come to him and make Our abode with him"* (JOHN 14:23). Obeying His Word leads to closeness in relationship. Not only does it draw us closer to both the Father and the Son, it frees the Holy Spirit to communicate with us (v. 26). Thus the whole Trinity is involved in speaking to any believer who prioritizes obedience—obedience that is motivated by love for the Lord.

The goal of love is obedience. The more you love someone, the more you want to please them. The more you want to please them, the more intimate your relationship grows. The more intimate your relationship grows, the freer the other person feels to speak with you. Legalism—where people obey only out of force or threat, out of fear or obligation—never works. It never leads to a higher level of hearing from God. Communication is a relational issue in which love drives our obedience.

Here's another illustration to drive home the point: A woman was married to a man who gave her a list of twenty-five demands he expected her to fulfill as his wife. He would regularly check the list to see if she was meeting his expectations. But the two of them rarely spoke or felt close to one another because their relationship was based primarily on rules. After a time, the man passed away. A year or so later, this widow fell in love and married someone else. One day as she was cleaning the house, she opened a drawer and ran across the list of duties her first husband had given to her—tasks she once hated. Seeing the list again brought a knowing smile to her face. Now, she was completing the entire list for her new husband and enjoying every minute of it. She was obeying from love now, not duty, and the result was a relationship in which they shared everything together.

The further we drift away from God, both in love and obedient lifestyle, the less we will hear Him. Coming near, loving to obey Him, invites the intimacy of hearing His voice.

The Holy Spirit

Galations 5 *Colossans*
WEEK TWO *3:12-18*

"This is My beloved Son . . . _Listen_ to Him!" **MATTHEW 17:5**

The _Holy Spirit_ is the primary way that you hear from God. *Ephesians 1:13 16-20*

The Holy Spirit is your _seal_.

"If the sin of Old Testament times was the rejection of God the Father, and the sin of New Testament times was the rejection of God the Son, then the sin of our times is the rejection of God the Holy Spirit."[1]

STEPHEN AND DAVID OLFORD *Soul*

The Holy Spirit is your _pledge_ *2 Corin MATT 6*

Every human being—saved or unsaved—is made up of three parts— _body_, _soul_, and _spirit_.

If the Holy Spirit lives in you, you haven't been _changed_, you have been _exchanged_

Relationship is the prerequisite for _recognition_ of God's voice. *Romans 10 9-10*

A "red light" of conviction is His way of saying "_stop_."
The "yellow light" of dis-ease means "_wait_."
A "green light" of ease and peace is His way of saying "_go_."

Acts 23 *Romans ch 9:1* *1 Corinthians 2 6-13*

Video sessions available for purchase at
www.LifeWay.com/DiscerningTheVoiceOfGod.

WEEK TWO

39

2 Timothy 1:3

HIDING IN PLAIN SIGHT

"God makes His desires known to those who stop at His Word, look in with a sensitive spirit, and listen to others. When we go to His Word, we stop long enough to hear from above. When we look, we examine our surrounding circumstances in light of what He is saying to our inner spirit (perhaps you prefer to call this your conscience). And when we listen to others, we seek the counsel of wise, qualified people."[2]

—CHARLES R. SWINDOLL

My father was always very playful. He'd often toss us down on the bed, grab hold of our ribs or anywhere else that he could get under our skin, and tickle us to high heaven. We'd gasp for air and scream for mercy.

In the fall, whenever he raked the leaves, he'd set aside a pile for the sole purpose of our jumping pleasure and usually jump in right along with us.

And then there was hide-and-seek.

He was never too good at hiding. We could always find him easily. He could never be quiet enough or stay concealed enough to keep us from discovering him with little effort. *"Da-ad, we can see you!"* we'd yell at the first sign of his foot or shirttail sticking out from behind the furniture. *"You're terrible at hiding!"* He'd laugh, let us find him, and then throw us to the floor and tickle us again.

As a mother with children of my own now, I realize what my sweet father was doing. I can see why he selected such prominent "hiding places," leaving hints and traces of his whereabouts. He wasn't hiding *from* us, seeking to frustrate and confuse us. He was hiding *for* us, giving us the joyful blessings of discovery.

Your *heavenly* Father does this too. He loves you so deeply that even when He seems elusive and distant, He's not. His affection for you compels Him to leave hints of His holiness and faithfulness to help lead you to Himself. You can be sure He will show you glimpses of Himself that will leave you marked forever.

He wants to be discovered.

HE SPEAKS

Throughout the Bible, God always made sure His children could discover Him and know His will. He was lovingly intentional about it. Deliberately strategic. While His primary *method* of communication shifted from one age to the next, His *purpose* did not.

The primary _____ God uses to speak to His

children has changed, but His _____ has not.

How would you summarize God's goal in speaking to His children?

> "Ask, and it will be given to you; seek, and you will find; knock, and it will be opened to you."
> MATTHEW 7:7

Our Father's goal has always been to reveal Himself in every age. In each time period, He has chosen the best method of communication to facilitate this glorious purpose. People in the Old Testament relied on prophets, signs, visions, and other external factors. With the coming of Jesus Christ followed by the Holy Spirit, God's primary method of speaking shifted in New Testament times.

In the previous paragraph, underline some of the primary ways God spoke in the Old Testament.

Below, you'll find specific examples of times when God revealed Himself and His plan in the Old Testament:
- Angels (Dan. 8:15)
- Burning bush (Ex. 3:4)
- Casting lots (Jonah 1:7)
- Cloud (Ex. 13:21)
- Dreams and visions (Num. 12:6)
- Fire (Deut. 5:25)
- Handwriting on a wall (Dan. 5:5)
- Theophany* (Judg. 6:12)

*"Theophany" refers to moments in the Bible when God Himself appeared in a physical manifestation.

- Urim and Thummim (Ex. 28:30)
- Visible signs (Judg. 6:40)

Turn in your Bible to Hebrews 1:1-4. Read it through carefully. Below, record the primary way God chose to speak, beginning with the Gospels?

Now read John 16:13 and Romans 8:14 in the margin. How do these verses suggest God began speaking primarily to His people beginning in the book of Acts until the present?

> "But when He, the Spirit of truth, comes, He will guide you into all the truth; for He will not speak on His own initiative, but whatever He hears, He will speak; and He will disclose to you what is to come."
>
> JOHN 16:13

Ah, the Holy Spirit.

In the Old Testament, the Holy Spirit was only given to specific people for a specific period of time in order to achieve specific tasks; this is also known as *selective indwelling*. Old Testament followers of God needed external means as the primary method of hearing Him (prophets, visions, and such) because they didn't have continuous access to the Holy Spirit.

> "For all who are being led by the Spirit of God, these are sons of God."
>
> ROMANS 8:14

Think back to Saul whose downward path as Israel's first king was marked by the chilling verse that said *"the Spirit of the LORD had left"* him **(1 SAM. 16:14, CSB)**. Remember Samson—shorn of his hair—thinking he could overpower his enemies as he had always done before, *"but he did not know that the LORD had departed from him"* **(JUDG. 16:20)**. Remember David appealing to God for forgiveness from adultery and murder, asking God to not *"take Your Holy Spirit from me"* **(PS. 51:11)**. God's people in the Old Testament would've given their left arm for the 24/7, whole-life access to the Holy Spirit that we as believers in this age enjoy.

How does John 14:16 describe our relationship with God's Spirit? How is this distinct from that of Old Testament believers?

How does Ephesians 1:13-14 confirm the constant presence of the Holy Spirit within those who've been redeemed?

Direct, personal access to God. Not selective. Not intermittent. Internal. And permanent. He loves you so radically, so graciously, that He has given you the promise of His presence. Access to the Holy Spirit is not an inferior, substandard alternative to prophets, signs, visions, and miracles. It is better—it is awesome.

Notice this: People in the Old Testament had no doubt that God had spoken to them. They weren't confused as to what He was asking them to do. The Father's intention remains the same today. He's not hiding from you now, same as He wasn't hiding from them then.

I admit I've often felt as though God was hiding from me. It seemed to me if He really wanted to be heard, He'd be more conspicuous and clear. I mean, He is after all—*God.* He can do whatever He wants. When I needed to hear Him, I would sometimes secretly wish for (and even pray for) a visible sign, like the cloud that led the children of Israel by day or the pillar of fire by night. I wanted a dove to supernaturally descend from the heavens at a particular time on, say, Tuesday if He was answering my request a certain way. Physical signs seemed to be the most unmistakable way of knowing God's voice.

But, alas, I saw no doves. No lightning strike from the skies. Why? Because He has provided a far superior means for us to be engaged in relationship with Him than our forefathers experienced. He has given us Himself, *permanently and internally*, in the Person of the Holy Spirit.

If you've come to this study discouraged because God always seems difficult to hear, remind yourself of His intention. Trust His heart. He's not hiding *from* you. He's hiding *for* you. He is leaving traces of His glory and glimpses of His grace like bread crumbs for you to follow. Remember, even the crumbs are important and intended to nourish you in a necessary way. Seeking is not worthless but rather a valuable part of your journey. The process itself is a way in which God can and does speak to us—maturing, molding, and strengthening us for His purposes.

In your group discussion time, consider how the need for external signs may correspond to a weakened faith. Conversely, consider how spiritual growth and maturity lead to a deeper reliance on the internal witness of the Holy Spirit. The following Scriptures will help facilitate your conversation.

- John 20:26-29
- Hebrews 2:3
- 2 Peter 1:16-19

SIGNS AND WONDERS

Let's be clear: Our God still works miracles and manifests Himself in tangible ways when He so chooses. He works signs and wonders even in this age. God still does the unusual, acting in supernatural ways whenever He wants.

I don't say this based solely on testimony I've heard from others. I've literally seen the jaw-dropping evidence of it for myself.

Yet, in hearing God, I haven't normally heard Him in miraculously visible ways. I've never heard an audible voice, for example, or seen a donkey open his furry mouth and speak the English language to me. (Thank the good Lord.) But I'm not arrogant enough to tell you what God would *never* do. I will not let my experience represent the full measure of how He is capable of acting. He alone can choose how He speaks to us. In any area of theology, unless the Scripture clearly teaches otherwise, we must leave room for God to be God.

When I use the word sensational, *I'm referring to ways that can be detected through the five physical senses.*

However, when He does choose to speak in *sensational* ways today, I can say with a fair amount of certainty on the authority of His Word—it will not serve as the foundation for us to hear from God but as confirmation of the Holy Spirit's leading and the message of Scripture.

Underline the two highlighted words in the last paragraph. Describe the difference between the two.

Why do you think it's critical to keep these two features distinct when attempting to accurately hear God? What kinds of faulty directions can occur if they're switched?

Answer the following statements as true (T) or false (F).

T | F   1. God can speak using any method He chooses.

T | F   2. God usually speaks today through visible signs.

T | F   3. God chooses to speak to me predominantly through His Spirit and His Word.

T | F   4. If God uses some sensational means to speak, I should rely on them above what the Spirit has revealed in Scripture.

T | F   5. If God uses sensational means to speak to me, they will only confirm what His Word and Spirit say.

One of the biggest challenges and joys of my life was being cast in a little, as yet unknown movie called *War Room*. I'd never considered acting on the big screen, and I was extremely intimidated by the idea when they called me completely out of the blue. In fact, when the producers called, I gave them several suggestions for qualified actresses who could play the role of Elizabeth Jordan much better than I. Still, they asked me to prayerfully consider it and at least look at the script. What I read on those pages sealed my decision. This wasn't a *movie*. It was *ministry*.

None of us involved in the film could have predicted it would climb to the number-one slot in the box office or become one of Sony's top-grossing films that year. Even more incredible was how the strength of this movie made the power of prayer a topic of national conversation. To this day, people still send me photos of personal prayer rooms they've created in their homes. People still tell me of their renewed emphasis on prayer after seeing *War Room*.

Months later, I remembered something that made the hair on my arms absolutely stand on end.

I was flipping through my journal, looking back at some notes from a Bible study I'd attended nearly eight years before the movie filming. The first day of the study, the teacher (who I'd never met before) looked my direction and said, "I just feel compelled to tell you that the Lord will do something through your life that will compel people to recognize and utilize the power of prayer." Then he added this: "It won't be only a few people who are affected. Many thousands will be inspired to pray."

I had no idea what he meant. Likely neither did he. All I know for sure is that in that moment my heart burned within me. His words resonated with the internal witness of the Holy Spirit. I knew for sure the Lord was speaking to me.

You'll never hear me say God doesn't speak in miraculous ways today. I've seen the proof of it more than once. I've seen His providential hand at work in circumstances, aligning events and orchestrating divine encounters. But hear me: I've learned not to *rely* on these instances. Miraculous occurrences don't replace God's Spirit as the chief means I depend on to hear His voice. He has not promised to lead us in a way that appeals to our senses; rather, He has promised to lead us in a way that appeals to our spirits—the leading of the Holy Spirit within us.

When God shows up in a tangible, surprising way, enjoy it, celebrate it, and thank Him for it. Then, turn your attention inward again, look to the Spirit and the Scriptures, and thank Him for giving you the most miraculous means of all for hearing His voice.

He has not promised to lead us in a way that appeals to our senses; rather, He has promised to lead us in a way that appeals to our spirits—the leading of the Holy Spirit within us.

HEARING THE HOLY SPIRIT

"A seared conscience is the sinner's heritage. It is upon this that the Holy Spirit first lays His hand when He awakens the soul from its sleep of death. He touches the conscience, and then the struggles of conviction come. He then pacifies it by the sprinkling of the blood, showing it Jesus and His cross. Then giving it the taste of forgiveness, it rests from all its tumults and fears."[3]

—HORATIUS BONAR

At the end of Jesus' earthly ministry, He told His beloved disciples that they would be better off after He was gone.

> "Nevertheless, I am telling you the truth. It is for your benefit that I go away, because if I don't go away the Counselor will not come to you. If I go, I will send him to you."
> **JOHN 16:7, CSB**

I'm sure we can't begin to imagine how devastated His disciples felt at this news. He'd hinted at it before, but they'd not wanted to believe it. In the grave finality of this moment, however, Jesus left no doubt about His soon departure. Yet the Holy Spirit, Jesus told them, would be a constant source of companionship and guidance in their lives after He was gone. The Spirit would reveal the mind of God to them, continuously and individually, and to each person who believed in Him.

Think back to yesterday's lesson and describe the differences between the way God guided Old Testament believers and how He chooses to lead us today.

"Now God has revealed these things to us by the Spirit, since the Spirit searches everything, even the depths of God."
1 CORINTHIANS 2:10, CSB

Do you remember why this is to our advantage? Summarize your answer here.

Since God's Spirit is the primary way we detect the Lord's leading in our lives, we must become better acquainted with how He works within us. The truths I'm about to share with you are breathtakingly exciting. Internalizing them will unlock your ability to discern God's voice.

Ready? Let's go.

> On the diagram below, write a capital letter S inside the smallest of the three circles. *(You'll be covering up the words "Human Spirit" that are already printed there. This is intentional. I want you to see the large "S" overtaking it.)*

Every human being has a *spirit*.* It is the core and inmost essence of a person. The human spirit was designed for relationship with God. If not divinely connected to Him in this way, we're left with a vacuum that can never be properly or completely filled. Like an intricately designed puzzle piece, the only true fit is the one true God.

*Note: As with many of the deeper things of God, humans have limited understanding as to how God created our souls and spirits. Scholars maintain varying views as to the delineation between spirit and soul. We'll prayerfully use this model for our purposes here to try and know God and His design more deeply.

When you became a believer in Jesus, the Spirit of God took up residence in your human spirit. Here, at your core, you were made brand new. (See 2 Cor. 5:17.)

I specifically asked you to draw a *capital* letter S inside this circle to represent God's Spirit. He is different and distinct from the human spirit. He is the third Person of the Trinity. The *human* spirit is a facet of humanity, but the *Holy* Spirit is the presence of God Himself.

> How would you explain the difference between the human spirit and the Holy Spirit to someone else?

> Go back to the diagram and look at the different elements that comprise your *soul*. What are they?
> 1.
>
> 2.
>
> 3.

> There's one missing element in the diagram. Below the other words in the darkened circle that represents the soul, write "conscience," and add it to your list above.

Every human being has a *soul*. It houses several critical facets of what makes each person unique: mind, emotions, ambitions, personality, things like that. In the soul there's also a deep inner voice called a *conscience*. This is an innate gut-level reaction that helps guide and direct each person's choices. It's an intrinsic response that should steer toward morality and goodness and away from danger and evil.

A conscience allows people who aren't Christians to still be moral, law-abiding, kind, and compassionate people. Some of the most thoughtful and considerate men and women I've ever known have been unbelievers. Why? The main reason: All people—Christian or not—possess a conscience. If their consciences have been stewarded well and trained well by parents, teachers, and other influencers, they are generally motivated to make the right choices.

Here's the problem: The conscience is only trustworthy up to a point.

We cannot follow our consciences as the sole basis for living because, apart from a relationship with Jesus, the elements in every person's soul are darkened and spiritually dead. They are dependent on environmental influences instead of spiritual influences to help shape and mold them. The conscience is formed and developed based on personal atmosphere and life circumstances—as distinct and individual as our fingerprints. Each person's conscience has been shaped by what it's been exposed to—whether that be traditions or deceptions, truth or lies.

This is why one person's conscience allows them to feel free to do something that another person's does not. I've known some individuals whose consciences held them hostage to a legalistic standard that's not in line with the freedom God offers them. Others feel fine participating in all manner of illegitimate activities without any internal conviction or warning. Unsteady and unpredictable factors determine the sensitivity of the conscience. Different for you than for me. Different for any one of us than for everybody else.

For example, Dorenda grew up in an environment where living together before marriage was not only tolerated but encouraged. "How else," they said, "would you know if you're compatible with a potential spouse? You have to try them out for a while!" Most everyone in her family has chosen this route to find a suitable partner. Dorenda feels little, if any, sense of discomfort or regret about her choice to move in with her current boyfriend. In fact, she feels quite comfortable and at ease with the decision. This is the norm in her family, and this norm has informed her conscience.

Dorenda's story illustrates how our consciences can be shaped in a way that's not pleasing to the Lord. Since our consciences are so *loud* inside us, we can easily mistake them for God's voice and leading in our lives. In order to hear Him clearly, we need our consciences awakened.

Name an example from your own life that illustrates this same point—an area in which your conscience has not been shaped in agreement with God's Word.

What have you done to retrain your conscience in this area?

AWAKENING THE CONSCIENCE

Be careful to remember this: your conscience *is not* the voice of God. But, your conscience can be used by the Holy Spirit as a type of microphone to amplify the volume of God's voice and to therefore guide you toward His direction for your life. However, this guidance requires a specific progression of events. Let's talk about that.

The human conscience _____ the voice of God.

When you became a Christian, your spirit became new. You weren't *changed* as much as you were *exchanged*. Something brand new came inside you. The Holy Spirit moved in. He gave you new life. (See Titus 3:5-7.)

Awareness of this truth is the first step toward more clearly hearing God. If the human conscience (or any other element of our souls, for that matter) has any chance of reflecting the light of Christ, it must first be brought from death to life. This can only happen when the Holy Spirit is within us. He must indwell your human spirit.

When I became a Christian, I didn't become

_____. I became _____.

Now that you've been exchanged as a believer, your human spirit is filled by the Holy Spirit. The capital-S Spirit. And (here's where it gets really good) God's Spirit doesn't remain confined to that small center in the diagram. His influence in your *spirit* begins to spill out into your *soul*, not only awakening it from spiritual slumber but also progressively conforming it into the image of Jesus Christ. (See 2 Pet. 1:3-4.)

A CONSCIENCE CAN BE . . .

- Blameless
  (Acts 24:16)

- Clear
  *(1 Tim. 3:9;
  2 Tim. 1:3)*

- Corrupted
  (Titus 1:15, NIV)

- Defiled
  (Titus 1:15)

- Evil
  (Heb. 10:22)

- Good
  *(Acts 23:1;
  1 Tim. 1:5,19;
  Heb. 13:18)*

- Guilty
  (Heb. 10:22, NIV)

- Seared
  (1 Tim. 4:2)

- Weak
  (1 Cor. 8:7,10,12)

Conviction refers to a sense of internal discomfort that leads toward a desire to change your behavior.

Grab a colored pen or highlighter and go back to your three-circle diagram (p. 48). Fill in the center circle over the capital letter S, and then let the color seep over into the next circle as well. *Remember your kindergarten teacher telling you to always stay within the lines? Ignore her. Be a little messy.*

This is a picture of what's happening in your life, even as you participate in this Bible study. As you surrender your life to God and obey His written Word, the influence of the Spirit is spilling over into the realm of your soul, awakening your conscience. And then—

A steady, progressive reprogramming and reformatting process begins. Over time, your Spirit-led conscience becomes remolded into the image of Christ, able to be used like a microphone for the Holy Spirit to speak to you—convicting you, challenging you, and guiding you toward God's will for your life.

> Look up John 16:8. What types of direction does the Holy Spirit offer to an *exchanged* believer?

After salvation, because of the Holy Spirit, certain kinds of activities, thoughts, or attitudes don't feel comfortable to you anymore, even if they did before. Something you may have once done without concern now feels wrong and problematic—increasingly so over time. Participating in certain behaviors, entertaining certain habits, engaging in certain relationships may become awkward and difficult with little apparent reason. Other than this: God's Spirit is infiltrating your soul—influencing you, molding you. Your conscience is being conformed into the image of Christ.

Don't fight against this process. Embrace it. It's the first step to hearing God clearly.

List three examples of an attitude or action you felt convicted about *after salvation* that you would never have felt uneasy about *before salvation*.

Did you credit this change to the Holy Spirit? If not, why did you think this was happening? How did you respond?

We'll come back to the other elements of your circle diagram later this week. For now, I want you to simply recognize and rejoice in the miraculous work of God in giving you the indwelling Holy Spirit to awaken your conscience and mold it into a—yes, a microphone! Knowing the changes you may be sensing are a sign of the Holy Spirit's presence in you, be especially mindful of how you choose to respond and react to them.

In fact, pause here and think about what your intuition/gut/conscience *feels* like. Even before you became a Christian, even before your inner sense of warning or guidance was being influenced by the Holy Spirit, how did your conscience *feel* to you?

Try to describe that feeling in this space.

Keep that feeling in mind—it's similar to the feeling of hearing and sensing God's conviction and direction.

CHECKS AND BALANCES

"I know the Lord is speaking to me when I have peace, God's Word confirms it, godly people in my life who know me best affirm it. And, my wife agrees!"

—ROBERT MORRIS

Everybody wants to be good at what they do. Everybody wants to be excellent in areas that are important to them. When the curtain's up, when the call to action comes, when you're expected to perform—at home, at work, in stressful situations—you want to be able to hit it out of the park.

Not everybody, however, wants to practice.

Hearing from God, like everything else, takes practice. Since your conscience is not the voice of God, hearing Him requires a trained ear. Even though your conscience is influenced by His Spirit, it is still a human component. It's fallible. As we're surrounded on all sides by a noisy, distracting, disorienting world, being clear on what God is saying to us is rarely a simple task.

It takes practice. It only gets easier with practice.

The following five practice drills have been a lifeline for me in gaining clarity on God's direction. I'm praying they'll serve the same purpose for you. Together, they put some protective measures in place that will help make sure you are hearing your Spirit-led conscience accurately. Even when you sense conviction or a deep knowing regarding some area of your life, these checks and balances may keep you from being led astray.

I call them the "Five Ms of Correctly Hearing God." Here they are:

1. LOOK FOR THE *MESSAGE* OF THE SPIRIT. Intentionally listen. Be still and consciously turn your attention inward to see if what you're sensing carries the weight of God or is simply the fleeting, unsteady voice of your own emotions. Don't just casually ask God for guidance. Discernment like this takes time. And patience. And practice.

2. LIVE IN THE *MODE* OF PRAYER. Don't talk to others about anything more than you talk to God about it. Submit anything you think you're hearing from Him back to Him in prayer. When the issue comes into your mind throughout the day, don't waste time worrying. Instead, spend your time handing the issue over to God.

3. SEARCH OUT THE *MODEL* OF SCRIPTURE. Carefully consider what the Bible says. Dig into the Word and find out. Does what you think you're hearing contradict the character of God or His Word in any way? If it does, guess what—you're not hearing God correctly.

4. SUBMIT TO THE *MINISTRY* OF ELI. Just as this priest of Israel provided young Samuel with insight as to how to recognize the voice of God (1 Sam. 3), seek the counsel of a wise, more mature believer who is practiced in discerning God's voice in his or her own life.

5. EXPECT THE *MERCY* OF CONFIRMATION. Ask the Lord to confirm His internal Word with external evidence. He desires for you to know His will. He's not hiding it from you. He will graciously verify His message through His Word, through circumstances, or even through another person.

We will never arrive at some mystical place of spiritual perfection. We will always make mistakes. *(Yes, expect to be mistaken sometimes in discerning the voice of God.)* But, He knows your heart and intention. He knows your desire to hear Him accurately and follow His guidance. If we refuse to obey an impression from God because we're too afraid to risk making a mistake, we'll miss the chance to walk in victory or experience the joy of relationship with Him. In fact, mistakes are often the greatest teachers to help us learn to discern Him more clearly in the future.

So, practice. Stub your spiritual toes and scrape your spiritual knees. And once you're back on your feet, start practicing again. Every time you do, you're training your spiritual "senses" (Heb. 5:14). You're growing. You're maturing. That's what the Five Ms are for.

The Five Ms are so important that I want you to go back and read them again. Then, rewrite each of the main principles in your own words below.

1.

2.

3.

4.

5.

Which of these steps have you not been doing?

Which *have* you been doing? How have they helped you?

TRANSFORMATIONS

Being a proactive seeker of God and submitting yourself to His will can feel like a scary task. What if He tells you to do something you've always resisted? What if He tells you to walk away from something you've always enjoyed? What if the thing *He* wants for you contradicts what *you* want for *you*?

Trust me, I get it. I recall my initial resistance to the thought of home-schooling my children, for example. Only wonderfully put-together women are organized enough for that task, right? I admired my older sister for doing it. I saw the value in it. I applauded friends and peers who'd chosen it. But it wasn't for me. Or so I thought.

Time passed. Our situation changed. And though no one was more shocked than I was, I began to feel drawn toward it. I even began to feel a sense of delight, excitement, and peace about it. By the time Jerry and I accepted that God was leading us in this direction (the "ministry of Eli" was a big help here), the desires of my soul were in alignment with what God was saying. It's what I now *wanted* to do.

> Name one thing you never thought you'd enjoy or even be able to tolerate that God's Spirit later turned your affections toward.

I'm not suggesting that moving forward with decisions like these comes without challenge and struggle. It often does. The presence of difficulty doesn't necessarily mean you're making a mistake. It can often indicate you're on exactly the right path—that the enemy is resisting your progress toward God's best.

I'm also not suggesting that your feelings need to align before you move forward in obedience. If His Word is clear on something, you obey it whether you feel like it or not, whether it is simple or not.

But, sometimes God does allow our passions to be an indicator of His direction. If you're delighting in Him (Ps. 37:4), He will often stir your heart, redirecting your feelings and desires in a certain way. When you sense an about-face in your interests, perhaps one that is even surprising to you, tune in.

Again, becoming more acquainted with this type of listening takes practice. But the more you pay attention and do it, the more adept at it you'll become. If you really want to get good at it, I suggest you start by disciplining yourself to do what you already *know* God's will for your life to be. That's what we'll finish today's study discussing.

HIS JOB, YOUR JOURNEY

The book of James was written to believers whose human spirits already had the big S written across them. They'd already been made new through salvation. Yet he said to them, *"Putting aside all filthiness and all that remains of wickedness, in humility receive the word implanted, which is able to save your souls"* (**JAS. 1:21**).

What seems a bit awkward, if not flat-out surprising, about the last portion of this verse?

Weren't they already saved? Why did their "souls" still need to be saved? Answer: Despite the rebirth of our human spirits, our souls (as well as our bodies) still contain *"filthiness and all that remains of wickedness."* Our *spirits* are saved, but our *souls* and *bodies* still need some serious work.

> Our *spirits* are saved, but our *souls* and *bodies* still need some serious work.

Read 2 Thessalonians 2:13. (It's in the margin.) It gives this renovation process a name. In the margin, underline the theological term in this verse that describes this renovation process. Right after that, circle who's responsible for bearing the burden of this process.

What a relief! The burden of "sanctification" (that's the word I was looking for) doesn't fall to you. It falls to the Spirit (that's the other word I was looking for) to reshape and reconfigure your soul—your thinking, emotions, and desires. This change is not always comfortable, but it puts you in position to hear Him more clearly, to walk in obedience to Him, and to receive His blessing in your life. As the Spirit conforms you to the image of Christ, the gap narrows between *His* desires and *your* desires.

> "We should always give thanks to God for you, brethren beloved by the Lord, because God has chosen you from the beginning for salvation through sanctification by the Spirit and faith in the truth."
> **2 THESSALONIANS 2:13**

Even though sanctification is the Spirit's responsibility and specialty, you and I must cooperate with Him in this work. Each of the following verses reveals cooperative actions we must complete in our work alongside the Spirit as He sanctifies us. In fact, our participation accelerates our growth and helps make God's voice clearer in our spiritual ears.

> "I appeal to you therefore, brothers, by the mercies of God, to present your bodies as a living sacrifice, holy and acceptable to God, which is your spiritual worship. Do not be conformed to this world, but be transformed by the renewal of your mind, that by testing you may discern what is the will of God, what is good and acceptable and perfect."
> **ROMANS 12:1-2, ESV**

> "And do not grieve the Holy Spirit of God, by whom you were sealed for the day of redemption."
> **EPHESIANS 4:30, ESV**

"Therefore put away all filthiness and rampant wickedness and receive with meekness the implanted word, which is able to save your souls. But be doers of the word, and not hearers only, deceiving yourselves."
JAMES 1:21-22, ESV

In your own words, rewrite the five highlighted portions in these previous verses.

1.

2.

3.

4.

5.

Are you doing these things? If not, why not? Why waste any more time? God wants to speak. Don't you want to hear? It's practice time! So when the game's on the line, you'll be ready—with God's instructions in hand.

In what ways are you cooperating with the Holy Spirit?

In what ways are you resisting?

FREEDOM TO HEAR GOD

I'm not a scientist. I've never looked into all of the biological ramifications of DNA and how it's shared between mother and child. But it does strike me as interesting that my oldest son loves chocolate, far more than his siblings do. I didn't have much interest in the stuff myself until I was eight months pregnant with him.

Seriously. Before then, if I wanted dessert, I would always lean toward the fruit option. (*"I'll have the apple pie, please."*) But, one day—literally, *one day*—I woke up, rolled my large belly into a somewhat more comfortable position, and suddenly *craved* chocolate! At my request (perhaps my demand), my sweet husband went to the store to get some delicious milk chocolate for his gargantuan wife. With that one gesture of unbridled kindness, a monster was unleashed.

So, no, I don't know all of the genetic terms to describe this phenomenon. But I do know this: the new life growing inside of me affected my taste buds. Now that my fourteen-year-old can make dessert choices of his own, it's interesting that our tastes are so similar.

When the new life of the Holy Spirit takes up residence in you, He begins to change your taste buds so that they mirror His. The DNA of God shows up in the fabric of your everyday life. That's just the way it is.

> Look up Hebrews 8:10 in your Bible. What does it say the Holy Spirit does with the Word of God?

LOOK HERE

One of the most freeing discoveries of my life has come from simply trusting that the divine DNA within me will naturally manifest itself through me. This single news flash has released me from the tedious, debilitating worry of "finding God's will for my life." When you and

I are looking around every corner to discover His will, worried to death that we're missing it or neglecting it, we can't freely engage in what He's put right in front of us to do. We end up missing His will because we're so busy searching for it!

Revealing insights from two verses in Philippians can set you free to enjoy your life with God while tuning your spiritual senses to hear His voice.

> In both of the following verses, underline the portion that indicates God's responsibility.

"It is God who is at work in you, both to will and to work for His good pleasure." **PHILIPPIANS 2:13**

"Let those of us who are mature think this way, and if in anything you think otherwise, God will reveal that also to you." **PHILIPPIANS 3:15, ESV**

Did you see it? The burden of responsibility for the *desire* and for the *energy* to engage in His will—it's His, not yours. (That's the Philippians 2:13 part.) Furthermore, if you step away from what God desires for you in any way, He will quicken your heart and let you know. (That's the Philippians 3:15 part.) The believers at Philippi did not have to walk around in constant dread, worrying that they were outside of God's will. Instead, they were to simply invest themselves fully in knowing Christ. And if they were out of alignment with Him, He would let them know.

God is already doing everything necessary not only to reveal His will to you but to cause you to go after it. Desiring and doing His will is not your responsibility to discover; it is His responsibility to reveal.

> Look up the following passages. Write out the portions that corroborate this principle.

1 Corinthians 12:6

We end up missing His will because we're so busy searching for it!

Desiring and doing His will is not your responsibility to discover; it is His responsibility to reveal.

Hebrews 13:20-21

James 1:17-18

In what current decision or other area of your life does this truth specifically and personally give you a sense of ease and peace?

Stop frantically searching for God's will; start frantically searching for God Himself.

Stop frantically searching for God's will; start frantically searching for God Himself. And as you do, trust that He will bear the responsibility to show you what He wants you to do and how He wants you to do it. He will speak through His Holy Spirit and His Word to reveal Himself to you, realign you to His perspective, and refocus you on His purposes. Do your part, and let Him do His.

What's the difference between seeking God's will and seeking God Himself?

What intentional practices could you undertake to set yourself on the right path of seeking God?

GROW UP

That son of mine who loves chocolate may have my tastes in desserts, but he's becoming his father's clone—not only in stature but in demeanor. His gestures, posture, and even his attitude and behaviors are a direct reflection of his dad.

Granted, some of these similarities have been learned over time as the boys have watched their father, probably not even realizing themselves how much they were studying the nuances of his behavior. But much of it is simply a genetic impartation, an outworking of their biology. Simply having his genetic makeup inside causes similar behaviors to manifest themselves outside. It's just how they've grown up.

It's happened naturally.

Go back to your spirit/soul/body diagram on page 48. Grab your highlighter again and extend the coloration into portions of the third, larger circle—the body. Then, meet me back here.

On the following list, circle the parts of your body that you most struggle to present to God as a living sacrifice.

- Mind (what I think about)
- Eyes (what I see)
- Hands (what I do)
- Mouth (what I say)
- Ears (what I listen to)
- Feet (where I go)
- Other _____

Why do you think yielding this area to God proves so difficult for you?

Rewrite some of the key phrases in Romans 12:1-2 as they appear in your Bible.

If you and I were doing this exercise together over a warm, sugary latte (I wish we were—we'd have so much fun), I'd have circled the word *mouth* for sure. Then, I'd tell you how, growing up, I was a docile,

"I believe in the truth found in Romans 12:1-2. If I have presented my body to Him as a living sacrifice (and I have), and I'm being transformed by the renewing of my mind, then I'm able to prove—to put to the test—what His will is. He will show me that which is good, acceptable, and perfect for me."

KAY ARTHUR

meek child who was admirably respectful of authority and mindful of every word that proceedeth forth from her mouth.

Then I'd pause and wait for you to double over in laughter.

Indeed, my mouth has always gotten me into heaps of trouble. Still now. As an adult woman. Growing up, if I received a demerit at school, my parents wouldn't even need to ask what it was for. They knew. Inevitably it had something to do with my propensity to over-talk. If I was disciplined at home, it was always linked in some way to thinking before speaking — and how so often, I didn't think before speaking. Mastering and controlling my mouth (among many other things) has given the Spirit plenty to work on in my life. I know that God doesn't *"slumber nor sleep,"* but if He did, I'm pretty sure I'd have given Him reason to need a nap or two in my time **(PS. 121:4)**.

So *mouth* is my answer. What's yours?

No matter what you circled, the truth is we're both in the same boat. We're all in dire need of the Spirit's influence to manifest in our physical behaviors. *In our bodies.* The good news is that His work is not stifled beneath the skin, relegated to the intangibles of our lives (mind, will, emotions, conscience). His effect spins outward, seeping through our pores until His fruit is seen in the visible realms of our lives. Just as He works to close the gap between Himself and the elements of our soul, He also works to close the gap between Himself and our body.

Here's the freeing part. Just as the nuances in a baby's appearance and behavior mirror its DNA, a believer's behavior is naturally influenced by her spiritual lineage. So it's unnecessary (actually counterproductive) to focus solely on outward behavior. Instead, we should simply focus on being spiritually healthy. Health will naturally produce growth which will automatically lead to behavior that reflects your Father's DNA.

Write this progression in your own words.

Is there an area of life where you've been focusing on changing your behavior instead of maintaining healthy spiritual growth? Explain.

If so, how have you seen a converse effect that's actually hampered your development?

Using your own grit and personal resolution to force changes in your behavior is not only exhausting to maintain but nearly always proves to be nothing more than a temporary fix. Inevitable relapses churn up into a never-ending cycle of disappointment, frustration, self-hatred, along with other unhealthy emotions. Lasting change—the kind that frees you to walk within rhythms of grace, fueled by the power of God—must stem from the inside, not the outside. Despite your sinful deficiencies, which each of us shares, trust yourself to His care and cooperate with Him in the ways He's instructed. The DNA is there. Trust Him to fashion your behaviors in the image of Christ.

The Spirit's effect on our bodies is reiterated in 1 Thessalonians 5:23. Write the progression of the Spirit's influence, as seen in this verse.

The sanctifying of the _____ leads to the sanctifying of the _____ which leads to the sanctifying of the _____.

In order to get your whole being in alignment, able to hear God and obey Him across all systems and structures—spirit, soul, and body—we should maintain the posture that I once heard a missionary to Africa describe. Each morning, he said, immediately upon rising, he would stretch out across his bed, picturing it as an altar on which he was the sacrifice. Then, he would say, "Lord, this day I present myself as a tool for You. Today I am Your living sacrifice."

"If the Spirit of him who raised Jesus from the dead dwells in you, he who raised Christ Jesus from the dead will also give life to your mortal bodies through his Spirit who dwells in you."
ROMANS 8:11, ESV

"Now may the God of peace himself sanctify you completely, and may your whole spirit and soul and body be kept blameless at the coming of our Lord Jesus Christ."
1 THESSALONIANS 5:23, ESV

THE FIFTH DAY

Read 2 Corinthians 3:12-17 in your Bible and answer the following questions.

When the law of Moses was read under the old covenant, what effect did it have on the hearer (vv. 14-15)?

What is the only thing that can lift the veil of understanding (v. 16)?

The Word of God, given without the clarity of the Holy Spirit, will not penetrate the hearer's understanding. Only by His Spirit can the veil be lifted from our eyes so that we as believers can (1) understand God's Word and (2) put it into practice.

As a Christian, you've been given the right and privilege to do both of these things: hear and respond. The Holy Spirit within you is everything you need. Through His transforming influence, the elements of your soul—mind, will, emotions, conscience—can each begin to operate in conjunction with God's purposes as you yield yourself to Him. The elements of your physical body and outward behaviors too—as you lay those on the altar—become changed at their root level, not just cosmetically on the surface, so that your whole person is filled with spiritual health and able to bear spiritual fruit.

The Spirit is the difference. By God's grace, His Spirit is fully yours. Delight in Him. Rest in Him. Believe that He will speak clearly to you, order your steps, and cause you to desire what brings Him pleasure.

No longer must you frantically search for God's will. Frantically search for God.

He will be found. And you will be changed.

As before, feel free to use this Fifth Day to gather all of your week's experiences with the Lord—a tying-up of loose bundles of information, coming together in a way that truly nourishes and equips you for the coming days.

Consider spending this time focused on areas where you're sensing God leading you in directions that may go against the way you feel or where you're sensing a desire for something that you're not sure is God's desire. Flip back to page 55 where we discussed the Five Ms, and make today a practice session, employing any of these strategies as your means of seeking Him.

Even if you don't gain specific clarity today, the practice will still be worth it. You'll know you're moving in the right direction. You'll sense changes in how you're surrendering to Him, wanting nothing other than His will.

"Your labor in the Lord is not in vain."
1 CORINTHIANS 15:58, CSB

"Do not grow weary in doing good."
2 THESSALONIANS 3:13, CSB

THE HOLY SPIRIT IN ACTION

by Dr. Tony Evans

In the church age, the Holy Spirit is the assigned representative of the Trinity. He is the agent of revelation and illumination for the believer who lives in an abiding relationship with Christ (John 14:16-26). Just as the Holy Spirit oversaw the perfect recording of Scripture to protect it from error as it was being originally written (2 Pet. 1:19-21), He continues to illumine the Word in our hearts as if by turning up a dimmer switch—progressively increasing our accurate comprehension of God's written Word while enabling us to make relevant application of the Word to our personal lives and decisions. We need Him for both general understanding and specific direction.

Think of it like this: Football games function based on objective rules that govern how the game operates. Yet each team has the freedom to call specific plays based on changing situations. In similar manner, God's objective Word is the fixed standard by which we all live. The role of the Holy Spirit—like a divine play caller—is to provide individual guidance based on the changing realities of life, always based on God's unchanging Word. Just as a team's individual strategy must operate within the fixed rules of the game, the Spirit's voice will always operate within the boundaries of God's revealed Word.

The process by which the triune God communicates to believers is called *"the anointing"* (**1 JOHN 2:27**). Through the Spirit's indwelling presence, He does the work of clarifying, applying, and confirming the truth of God to us. This anointing is so powerful that John says it results in *"hav[ing] no need for anyone to teach you"* (**V. 27**). That is, you don't need to go to nonbelievers to gain spiritual understanding, insight, and direction. Just as you no longer need

a rabbit ear antenna to get television reception once you've established a satellite or cable hookup, believers who are operating in unity with God's Word must not resort to human wisdom—those who don't know God—in order to gain spiritual clarity. The Holy Spirit does it for us. Through Him, we have the anointing.

As Paul said, the Holy Spirit reveals God's truth to those who are spiritual, *"combining spiritual thoughts with spiritual words"* (**1 COR. 2:13**), and sharing them with spiritual people equipped to *"appraise"* what they are hearing (**V. 15**). Those who try listening by natural means, through the path of human wisdom, have no way of understanding God's truth. But, by having *"the mind of Christ"* (**V. 16**), our thought processes stay connected to what God has revealed in Scripture. When our thoughts are constantly aligned with God's revealed truth, the Holy Spirit can transfer the thoughts of God into our minds. Transformed thinking then results in transformed living (2 Cor. 3:17-18). That's how the Holy Spirit's voice truly changes our lives.

The Holy Spirit's Voice

WEEK THREE

HOLY SPIRITS VOICE   EPH 4: 22-23
   Col 3: 9-10

"But when He, the Spirit of truth, comes, He will __guide you into__ __all TRUTH__ ; for He will not speak on His own __self initiative__ *INITIATIVE* but whatever He hears, He will speak; and He will disclose to you what is to come." **JOHN 16:13**

The Greek word for guide means __to lead someone who is already on their WAY__ Or, a person who advises, points out, and shows others the way.[1]

1. He guides you __PROGRESSIVELY__

> ". . . so that we may know the things __Freely Given__ to us by God . . ." **1 CORINTHIANS 2:12**

> *If He gives us too much, we'll either* __RUSH__*impatiently toward it, or we'll be so intimidated by His assignment that we will _____ from it and run in the opposite direction.*

PS 37:4

2. He guides you __intentionally__.

3. He guides you __internally__. *LAYER*

> There is an __internal layer__ of __TRUTH__ that we do not have access to in our own human wisdom.

__STRONGhold__ stand against the knowledge of God.

DAY ONE

PERSISTENT:

A LIGHT UNTO MY PATH

"God's impressions within and His Word without are always corroborated by His providence around, and we should quietly wait until these three focus into one point.[2] . . . If you do not know what you ought to do, stand still until you do. And when the time comes for action, circumstances, like glowworms, will sparkle along your path. You will become so sure that you are right, when God's three witnesses concur, that you could not be surer though an angel beckoned you on."[3]

—F. B. MEYER

I wish you could see me right now. I'm sitting on an airplane flying home from a weekend of ministry in Florida. And I'm smiling—I mean, from ear to ear. Giddy with excitement about this third week of our study together, because so much of the clarity we need for hearing God's voice is going to unfold in these next few days. So, yeah, I'm smiling—thinking about your life exploding with victory as we go deeper together into this study, into the characteristics of God's voice that differentiate it from all the other errant voices seeking to keep you from doing what God wants you to do.

Oh, and speaking of airplanes—I'm intrigued that God would allow me to be sitting in this aluminum tube sailing through the heavens as I'm writing. In a couple of hours, this hulking mass of steel will be landing (safely, I'm hoping) back down on the planet. And I've gotta admit, I'm always a bit disturbed by this process—four hundred and fifty tons of heavy machinery, jet fuel, and human cargo hurtling at breakneck speeds toward the earth. I whisper a prayer every single time.

I've noticed, particularly at night, how the plane always touches down on a path that's been clearly outlined with lights. Not just *one* light. *Many* lights. All lined up in a row. They're unmistakable. Sure, the pilot's been informed by the control tower of his landing position. He's been given clear directions. But as confirmation of what he's heard, look what's on the ground in front of him—not just a single, solitary light for him to nose-dive toward. Not just a haphazard guess or a loose hope that it's the right one. No, he searches the landscape for a trail of consistent lights that match what he's been told in his earpiece.

The lights guide him home.

One of the distinguishing characteristics of the Holy Spirit's leading in your life is that it will be illumined by confirmations, divinely designed to help ensure that you are landing on the right pathway. His voice will be both consistent and persistent.

WHAT'D YOU SAY?

In order to confirm His leading—in order for us to more clearly discern His voice—the Holy Spirit deals with us in a patient, consistent, persistent fashion. He works in our hearts, in the hearts of others, and also in the events of our lives to point us in His direction. He uses all of these things to cause us to hear and heed His voice.

> In the sentence above, underline the three primary ways that God persistently solidifies His direction in your life.

> Remember the Five Ms of hearing God? From the third day of last week's lessons (p. 55)? Which one (or ones) does today's lesson explore?

> Recall a time when God "illumined your runway" so that you could be more certain you were landing on the right decision. What was His instruction about?

> List the ways that He confirmed it.

"For God speaks in one way, and in two, though man does not perceive it."
JOB 33:14, ESV

Did this choice affect other people in your life as well? If so, how did you sense an increased responsibility to accurately read these "lights" of confirmation?

When the prophet Samuel was only a boy, he worked in the tabernacle of God in Shiloh alongside Eli the priest. Once, in the dead of night, while Samuel was still in bed, he heard a voice calling out to him.

Open your Bible to 1 Samuel 3.1-10 and answer the following questions:

What factors could have made it difficult for Samuel to distinguish God's voice?

How many times did God call before Samuel recognized His voice?

Who did God use to help Samuel recognize His voice?

According to verses 19-21, what did Yahweh in His mercy continue to do even though Samuel had once taken a while to recognize and respond to God's voice?

The truths from this portion of Scripture make my heart pound in gratitude to the Lord for His patience and persistence. Samuel lived during an era when hearing God was a *"rare"* occurrence **(1 SAM. 3:1)**. He would not have been accustomed to the sound of God's voice. In fact, he may very well had never heard it before in his life. He was, after all, only a boy. Still, God spoke again and again, accommodating Samuel's immaturity and lack of experience. And God, *"being rich in mercy"* **(EPH. 2:4)** and knowing our weaknesses, will often pursue us again. And again. And again. He'll graciously give us continued opportunity to detect and discern what He is saying and respond in obedience.

How does being aware of God's persistence relieve any feelings of condemnation regarding your own growth and maturity in learning to hear God?

Let's look at one more passage. Turn to John 4:7-26, and dig into it for these observations:

How many times did Jesus speak to the Samaritan woman in this passage?

What words prove that she did not know she was speaking to the Messiah?

What words did Jesus use to clearly identify Himself?

Jesus was aware that this woman didn't know to whom she was speaking. And yet, instead of being offended at her lack of reverence for His deity, He entertained her questions and graciously engaged her concerns until her eyes were opened and she knew—*she knew*—the one speaking to her was indeed the Messiah.

Are you as encouraged by this as I am? Even with our propensity to not recognize His voice, He knows what's in our hearts, and He will consistently illumine our paths with internal inklings of the Holy Spirit, matching them with persistent, external confirmations that help make His voice clear to us.

SEEING THE LIGHT

People use the word *serendipity* to infer that the stars have aligned and the circumstances of their lives have pointed them in a single direction. The unbelieving person might also call it karma, fate, or coincidence. Palm readers and astrologists count on it for the foundation of their supposed business. But the believer knows that serendipity has nothing to do with astrology or numerology. In fact, the only role stars play is that of being the handiwork of the One who made them.

When wanting to know God's plan for your life, you're not looking for mystical signs detached from a living source. You're expecting God's continual confirmation of His will, deliberately given to you to help illuminate your path. When He speaks to you internally, and then causes other events to confirm what He's saying, it's not coincidence, luck, or chance. It is likely His sovereign hand orchestrating circumstances to help lead you to His will. When God speaks, He does so persistently.

Several years ago, I was asked to be part of a ministry project intended to emphasize the importance of prayer and hearing God, specifically through silence and stillness. As with every opportunity that comes into our office, my husband and I sought God's direction about whether or not to be involved. We didn't personally know the people who were producing this resource nor did we know some of the others who were slated to be part of it. We were a little concerned; but still, despite this lack of familiarity, we asked the Lord if we should participate.

Here's why: First, I was immediately intrigued by the topic. Something within me (I'll say *Someone*) caused me to initially respond with a keen sense of enthusiasm and passion. At the time, I was knee-deep in my own personal journey to really understand how to hear God and further develop my own prayer life. The disciplines of silence and solitude were currently at the forefront of my mind. In addition, many of the conversations I was having with mentors and friends, plus all of the books I was reading at the time, were specifically pinpointing these particularly important elements of our faith. The timing of all these things just couldn't be coincidental, could it?

To top it all off, the Sunday before we needed to determine whether we would say yes, a longtime trusted mentor sought me out before church service and told me she wanted to talk with me about how the discipline of prayer could be more effective and impactful in my life and ministry. She had no idea we'd been asked to do a project on this exact topic. She'd just felt compelled by God's Spirit to suggest it to me.

Count up these various confirmations with me. How many did you see?

What types of categories, activities, and other areas of life did they represent?

Why did it matter that I'd been noticing this?

That's not the end of the story. After the project was completed, we received many questions, concerns, and criticisms from people. And I don't mean a few. I'm talking about dozens. Most of them were from people who seemed to find joy in taking issue with things that were really non-issues. (You've met those kind of people before, haven't you?) Yet, even though the vast majority of these accusations didn't hold water, we were careful to consider everything that had been brought to our attention. We didn't want to enflame discord or ignore genuine problems that needed to be clarified. I remember shedding a tear or two in the process and losing a bit of sleep over it all.

After this inundation had gone on a while, my husband reminded me how diligent we'd been to seek God when this opportunity first came up. He recalled the persistent ways in which we'd seen His hand con- firming and leading us in the direction we chose. In that moment, a steady assurance flooded my heart—a strong sense of divine approval.

Because you know what? God *had* led us to that decision. Persistently. To the best of our abilities, we'd followed His voice. I knew that for sure. I'm not saying we couldn't possibly have heard Him wrong, but we'd definitely followed the runway lights before landing.

Even to this very day, if a question ever arises surrounding that project, I don't feel overcome with insecurity about it anymore—about whether or not I did the right thing. The Lord's *persistent* confirmations still assure me.

> Have you ever had a similar experience, where God's assuring confirmations quelled the criticism you may have received from others?

> Make a list below of the things God did or allowed to happen that confirmed His direction for you.

Distinguish between unnecessary criticisms and the wise advice of mentors and leaders. God's persistent assurance should help quell superfluous criticism, but His leading will be confirmed and highlighted by those who are legitimate spiritual authorities in your life. Let the advice of your mentors weigh heavily.

> How did these confirmations dispel the disapproval of others?

The Spirit speaks *persistently* because He wants you in line with God's will. As you patiently, prayerfully listen with a heart prepared to obey, you'll often notice a consistent pattern coming into view—a pattern that offers you a clear place to land.

PERSONAL:

HE KNOWS MY NAME

"I know the Lord is speaking to me personally when I read my Bible and a particular verse or passage seems illuminated—it just lifts up off the page, and I seem to hear a gentle, inaudible whisper as I have an 'aha moment' in my heart."

—ANNE GRAHAM LOTZ

My three boys are as different from one another as they can possibly be. Most of the time their father and I are stunned that they all came from the same two parents. Because their personalities and characteristics are so unique, we're consistently mindful of our need to parent them individually.

Like most parents, we try to operate with a collective set of guidelines. Many of the rules and privileges in our house apply to all the boys. But sometimes, one kid will need a more personalized, tailored approach to ensure he is *really hearing and understanding* what Jerry and I are trying to communicate. Seems like I'm always asking the Lord for discernment in knowing how best to motivate, train, and correct them. We need Him to help us know what makes each one of them tick and what communicates most clearly in that moment to that particular son.

When the Holy Spirit leads us, He not only does so *persistently*, but He also does it *personally* and *individually*. Sure, many of His directives are corporate in scope—designed for the entirety of the body of Christ. But He will often communicate personalized instructions as to how individuals need to carry out those corporate directives, based on the specific destination He has called them to reach.

The Holy Spirit leads me _____ and _____.

This feature of God's voice accomplishes two things: First, it gives us confidence that He knows us well enough to speak in a way we alone can hear. Secondly, it means we must be careful not to box others into a divine directive that was designed specifically for *us*.

The personal nature of God's voice accomplishes two things:

First, _____

Second, _____

CALLED BY NAME

I want you to launch into today's focus by honestly answering these questions. (I say "honestly" because most of us never admit some of these things out loud.) Check the appropriate box, and if you'd like, use the space provided in the margin to give a more detailed response.

○ YES ○ NO   Have you ever felt you needed to be more like someone else—maybe someone whose spiritual life you admire—in order to hear God?

○ YES ○ NO   Have you ever wondered if you needed to accumulate something more (more knowledge, more experience, more faith, more confidence, or whatever) in order to hear the voice of God?

○ YES ○ NO   Have you ever wondered if being a new Christian or being young in your spiritual development is what keeps you from being able to hear God?

○ YES ○ NO   Have you ever wondered if past mistakes could keep God from wanting to speak to you?

I suspect you answered yes to at least one or two of these hang-ups.

Many times in life, I've said yes to the first question. I've wished I was more like other believers whose relationships with God seemed more in-depth and intimate than my own. Comparison always leads to a sense of condemnation and hopelessness.

I've also felt the pressure of the second question. Many people equate higher learning with discerning spiritual ears. While age and theological knowledge may definitely assist someone in hearing God, neither of them guarantees it.

Regarding the third question, I've found that some of the hearts most tender toward God belong to new believers who are freshly aware of His Spirit, sensitive to His leading, and eager to obey.

What's more, in thinking through the last question, God knows where each of us is located on our journey with Him, and He can push beyond the white noise of our own environments, mistakes, and "what-ifs" to speak to us.

Did you notice in yesterday's lesson that when God spoke to the little boy Samuel, He called him by name? *"Samuel! Samuel!"* **(1 SAM. 3:10)**. When Jesus wanted to capture the attention of a weary woman seeking the body of her crucified Lord at the tomb, He said to her *"Mary!"* **(JOHN 20:16)**. Earlier He'd riveted the attention of a prospective disciple named Nathanael, displaying firsthand knowledge of him (John 1:47-48). And later, He astonished a determined man traveling to Damascus, calling to him from a blinding light, *"Saul, Saul"* **(ACTS 9:4)**, even though this religious zealot was a crusader against the rising swell of Christianity.

In each case, God showed that He *knew them*. Despite their situations and shortcomings, He knew how to heighten their abilities to discern Him. They weren't spiritual superstars. Some weren't even following Him yet, although He knew they eventually would. But no matter where they were—in a temple as a young child (Samuel) or sitting under the shading branches of a fig tree minding their own business (Nathanael)—He found them and spoke to them. *Personally*.

God's clear use of names and personal specifics when addressing these biblical characters gives us insight about the personal way in which He communicates. He has always intended His relationship with us to be a personal one, in which He "calls us by name," giving us detailed directions in accordance with what He wants to accomplish in our individual lives.

One word of caution, however. When this beautiful distinction of God's voice brushes up against the sinfulness in our hearts (our pride, jealousy, and judgmental attitudes) we can sometimes misappropriate His personal message in ways He doesn't intend.

○ YES ○ NO   Have other believers ever tried to hold you in
bondage to their own convictions?

If so, describe your experience below and be prepared to
share it with your small group. Be careful not to slander or
dishonor anyone in the process.

Yes, when God requires certain, specific things of us, we can easily
assume He must be requiring them of everyone else as well. If we
don't stand guard, we can become legalistic and judgmental, placing
other believers in bondage.

Certainly the Bible contains many black-and-white statements and
principles, things that apply at all times, in all places, to all people.
Truth is not relative. It's an objective standard. Any personalized directives He may call to your attention will never manipulate or pervert
His Word. Still, you cannot hold everyone around you to the same
personal application of truth to which God's Spirit has guided you. Or
use it to judge the seriousness of their devotion to Christ. Or feel sorry
for yourself because of what it's costing you personally.

If He's calling a younger woman to be a full-time mom, the Holy Spirit
may give her a personal conviction about not working outside the
home. If He's directing an older woman toward leading a Bible study,
He may give her a conviction about sacrificing certain legitimately
acceptable activities simply because they eat into her study and
preparation time. If He's speaking to anyone about tackling a spiritual need or struggle in his or her life or about adopting a long-term
prayer focus, He may convict that person to incorporate an extended
fast of some kind or to possibly rearrange work hours so they can
temporarily slice their day a different way.

Any promptings like these are specifically designed by God to foster
the needs of that man or woman *personally*. But while being diligent
to obey these leadings, he or she must resist the urge to errantly
become the Holy Spirit in the lives of others. God will direct those
people Himself.

In what ways have you felt tempted (or perhaps acted on the temptation) to impose a personal conviction on somebody else?

SAME DESTINATION, DIFFERENT DIRECTIONS

As God leads us in our journeys toward Him, we each follow different avenues. The Holy Spirit draws us individual maps to follow. Again, just to make sure I'm being clear: The authority of God's Word is universal and unquestioned. All roads do not lead to God or to obeying Him. But, inside of our personal relationships with Him, we'll find varied plans and pursuits that take into account His personal desires for us as distinct individuals.

Others may not choose to take our roads—and they *shouldn't*, if it's not part of their map. Nor should we challenge them regarding *their* routes, unless perhaps it's an issue of scriptural principle. We should give others the freedom to obediently follow the courses they've prayerfully determined are best for them.

Paul taught on this issue in Romans 14. The church in Rome was comprised of both Jews and Gentiles. Their different cultural upbringings brought divergent views on many things, including whether or not certain foods could be enjoyed. Paul used this as an illustration of how we should deal with our personal liberties and restraints as believers and how we should treat others who think differently than we do.

Based on Romans 14:1-6, mark each statement true (T) or false (F).

T | F   1. My response to those who hold opinions different from mine should be acceptance (v. 1).

T | F   2. God gives special favor to the one who chooses the action that appears to be most godly (v. 3).

T | F   3. I am not only accountable to my Master for my actions but also to other believers (v. 4).

T | F 4. As a Christian, I have a responsibility to judge others' actions (v. 4).

T | F 5. The only person who must be convinced about the actions I choose to take is me (v. 5).

T | F 6. The Holy Spirit could direct two people to do two different things, each equally glorifying to God (v. 6).

We don't change our convictions based on what others are doing. Neither do we judge others based on what He's personally asked of us. Convictions like these can be personal.

The Holy Spirit directs us according to His plan—a plan that could lead two believers in different directions, even though they equally love the Lord. As long as these actions fall within the guidelines of Scripture and as long as each person is following the Lord in obedience, both can bring glory to God. Our responsibility is only to be sure we are following God's leading in our own lives. *(Numbers 1, 5, and 6 above are true).*

Are you guilty of judging others based on your personal convictions?
○ YES   ○ NO   ○ I'M NOT SURE

If so, in the margin, list the initials of those you may have judged in this way.

Ask God for forgiveness for the judgment you have placed on them. As you offer each person to the Lord in prayer, place a line through his or her initials to symbolize a release from the bondage you've created. If your treatment has perhaps hurt someone in some way, prayerfully consider asking him or her for forgiveness.

God's Word and His truth are global and comprehensive. But the convictions He gives are often quite specific and personal. By learning to know the difference—both for yourself and for others—you'll live out His intended plan for *you* more freely.

HIS WORD:

A LAMP UNTO MY FEET

"I know the Lord is speaking to me when it is confirmed by Scripture. God has given us everything that pertains to life and godliness in His Word (2 Pet. 1:3). He never contradicts Himself and never acts contrary to His character."

—KAY ARTHUR

I was a broadcast journalism major at the University of Houston. During my sophomore year, one of my classes required each student to conduct an interview with an admirable personality in the community and write a story about them with journalistic integrity and detail. I dove into the task head-on, excited to get an interview with one of the city's top news anchors at the time, Melanie Lawson.

The day I walked into her office at the news station, I felt like a real live professional. I shook her hand, sat down in the cushioned chair opposite her desk, and grabbed the list of questions I'd prepared. She was kind and answered them one by one. I took notes but barely. Buoyed by youthful arrogance, I was sure I could retain the information mentally. I was too promising a journalist for such mundane tasks as tape-recording and tedious note-taking. *Pffsh.*

It wasn't until later, when I sat down at my dorm room desk to write the article, that I realized I didn't have nearly enough information to make ends meet. Tucking my tail between my legs, I called her back to re-ask a few questions. More than once, actually. After the second call, she scolded me—tenderly, but firmly—saying if I'd taken our meeting a bit more seriously, if I'd listened and kept better notes the first time, I wouldn't be in this situation.

She was right.

As the Lord has been teaching me to hear His voice, I am learning a similar lesson. The Bible is the primary channel through which He reveals His word and His assignments for me (for all of us). If I sit down with Him half-heartedly indifferent to what He's saying, I'm not likely to be left with the clarity I'll need later on. But if I value and prioritize meeting with Him, being careful to record and retain what He has *already said* in Scripture, I will find direction for my present and future circumstances.

Listen carefully: Scripture is the primary way God speaks. It is not only the main way you will hear Him, but it also provides the boundaries into which everything else He says to you will fall. If you ignore this chief means of divine communication, you will never hear God clearly.

Scripture is the _____ _____ God speaks, and it provides the _____ into which everything He says will fall.

Take a moment to digest these two layers of how God's Word helps us hear Him. Explain them further, in your own words, below.

HEARING THE WORD

Do you recognize the name of author Henry Blackaby. Yes? No? If you don't, you need to acquaint yourself with him, his writings, and his ministry as quickly as you can. His *Experiencing God* book and Bible study are a must. I've had the privilege of meeting with Dr. Blackaby twice. Gratefully, those two occasions were separated by enough years that he probably didn't realize I was asking him the same questions each time. Intrigued by his personal devotion and fervency for the Lord, I asked him to describe how he recognizes God's voice in his own life. He answered:

"It's really very simple. I always read the Word of God. The Holy Spirit uses the Word of God to bring me the mind and heart of God. When the Holy Spirit speaks through the Word of God, I always know that I have the will of God and can proceed."

There's so much wisdom in those simple words. You might want to read them again.

As you seek to hear the Holy Spirit speak through Scripture, you are tuning your spiritual ears to catch that moment when a passage, verse, or phrase—or even just a single word—grasps your attention in an almost shocking way, drawing your thoughts directly toward it and how it applies to a specific situation in your life.

The Holy Spirit orchestrates these events. *He speaks!* Oftentimes He speaks to simply spark you to worship, to recognize afresh some glorious facet of the gospel. At other times, a verse of Scripture may speak directly to a current event, crisis, or decision you need to make. In this way, the Bible is *"living and active and sharper than any two-edged sword"* **(HEB. 4:12)**. It pierces and penetrates, compels and convicts, directs and instructs, renews and redirects, changes and transforms—all at the same time. When you're reading the Scriptures and you feel a particular verse *grip you*, it's very likely the Holy Spirit speaking.

> Recall a time when a Scripture verse or passage seemed highlighted or personalized specifically for you. What did you do, if anything, to record or mark this moment?

> Underline the action verbs in the following verse:

> "But Mary treasured all these things, pondering them in her heart." **LUKE 2:19**

How could you begin to "treasure" God's Word to you?

Mark the moment. Throughout my Bible, I've written dates in the margin when and where the Lord used a verse to speak to me about something specific. Thumbing through, I am able to see a track record, a timeline, of God's Word that I can always refer back to.

We've lost the art of *treasuring* and *pondering*. I don't know exactly how Mary, the mother of Jesus, "treasured" the events surrounding her unexpected involvement with the Son of God, but the original wording here implies defending, preserving, and protecting.[4] She guarded what she gleaned about Him. She determined not to merely be awestruck and amazed by it, as others were (Luke 2:18), but to take it a step further and valiantly keep an account. She meditated on it, mulled it over, and tucked it away for safekeeping.

Sadly, our lethargic posture toward the wonder of God's Word is a major factor in our lack of hearing Him. When we hear His Word but do not treasure it as an irreplaceable keepsake, we miss out on its long-term benefits. The moment slips away. Then a month later, we can't remember the details of what we read and what was meaningful to us. *Do not let this happen.* Every time you detect the fingerprints of God orchestrating and intervening, every time you hear the weighty whisper of the Holy Spirit echoing in your heart, be quick to preserve it so that what He says cannot be easily forgotten.

Read each verse and then paraphrase it in the space provided.

John 16:13

2 Timothy 3:16

The Word is too valuable for us to let it escape unheeded—it's not just words. It is God speaking to you, guiding you *"into all the truth"* **(JOHN 16:13)**.

We have a friend whose wife is choosing to leave their marriage. She claims to have fallen in love with another man who makes her "happier" than her current husband. After a year of infidelity, both emotional and physical, she is convinced God is giving her His approval and—wait for it—His blessing to leave her "lackluster marriage for a more fulfilling relationship." She's told me that her choice is not only best for her but also for her current spouse and their family. She even quotes several verses that appear to corroborate her decision. Her conviction feels so deeply authentic to her that no amount of conversation can convince her that it is *not* God's Spirit giving her the freedom to move forward; though, she is obviously being led astray by the enemy's convincing deceptions.

Describe a time when you felt the desire to do something that contradicted Scripture.

> "Even Satan disguises himself as an angel of light."
>
> 2 CORINTHIANS 11:14

If, perhaps, you followed your own feelings or intellect instead of Scripture on this matter, what happened as a result? What might God have spared you from?

When you *did* follow Scripture, despite what you felt or thought, what happened from that obedience?

To those who are listening at all, hearing God's instructions on issues of principle where His will is explicitly expressed in the Bible (such as the marriage example I just gave) is quite obvious. But what about issues that are less black-and-white? Oh, the Scripture is your answer even then! It's not merely a reference book to search and slice by subject, to cut and paste into a formula. It is the living Word of God. The Spirit *speaks* through it, applying passages that at first may seem impersonal, irrelevant, or anachronistic in regard to our particular situation. In the light of His revealing guidance, they now seem pricelessly apropos.

Even God's personal word *will always fall within the boundaries of His* written Word.

This Book is *alive*!

SATURATED IN THE WORD

The more Scripture that's hidden in your heart, the more you are offering God an opportunity to utilize it in your life. This is one of the reasons why we should prioritize our time with Him. It is our daily bread—nourishing, encouraging, and refreshing us in every way. Through the Bible, we get to know God better and receive insights for living.

Rank the following daily activities from 1 to 10 with 1 being the thing you prioritize most and 10 being what you prioritize least. *(I've given you a blank spot, too, in case I've left off one of your priorities.)*

___ Watching television

___ Being attentive to spiritual matters (Bible study, prayer)

___ Reading magazines

___ Surfing the Internet

___ Escaping into novels

___ Working

___ Talking on the phone

___ Pursuing other hobbies

___ Spending time with family

___ Perusing social media

___ Something else _____

None of these activities is wrong, but what does your prioritization tell you about your regard for God and His written Word?

Most of us feel we don't have enough time to meditate on God's Word, but—let's be honest. We have time for anything we make time for. It all comes down to priorities. If you're serious about beginning to reprioritize God and His Word in your life, start here: Take one or two verses a week and write them on index cards. Duplicate them, and stick them in some of the more conspicuous places where you'll see them through the day—such as the wall of your office cubicle, your bathroom mirror, or the steering wheel of your car.

Our priorities are reflected in what we designate and treat as more important than another thing.

Every morning for seven days, immerse yourself in these verses—as you wash your face, brush your teeth, and go throughout your day. Ask the Lord to speak to you and teach you through His Word as you meditate on it all day long. Consciously bring these verses to your mind as you take part in your daily activities. Ask Him to show you how they apply to practical scenarios you face. By the end of the week—I guarantee—each of these verses will be inscribed on your heart and mind.

Choose two of the following verses to meditate on this week. Write them on cards, and display them where you will see them often.

- Psalm 25:14
- Psalm 27:13-14
- Isaiah 33:6
- Zephaniah 3:17
- Romans 8:35-37
- Galatians 5:1

Then, from week to week, just keep growing your collection of verses. There's always more. They'll never run out. A lifetime supply. A lifetime of hearing from God by listening to His Word.

PEACE:

HARMONY

In college I was part of a Christian sorority that provided an alternative for Christian women who didn't want to be involved with secular sororities. I enjoyed my time with this group. We shared a lot of good times. We had a lot of good experiences. I also chose to join another, more traditional sorority on campus. Many girls genuinely believed that joining a secular sorority displeased God. But me? I believed the Lord gave me freedom to do it if I wanted to. And I didn't really see (or care) how my decision might affect anyone else.

But it did. It raised some questions, especially among younger women in our Christian group, some of them fledgling believers who looked up to me. What I'd done really bothered them. It shook their confidence in me and in what I represented. Today, all these years later, I look back and see that my freedom created an unnecessary divide among sisters. For this reason, it was the wrong choice to make. And if I'd been listening for the voice of God, rather than placating my own pride, I would have placed more priority on harmony among friends. I'd have seen the discord my decision was creating and taken it as my cue not to move forward.

Because it disrupted our peace.

Peace is an important facet to accurately hearing God because He desires unity and mutual edification within the body of Christ. Scripture urges us to be *"diligent to preserve the unity of the Spirit in the bond of peace"* **(EPH. 4:3)**. We're to *pursue* peace with others.

> In your own words, what makes peace such a high-value commodity among the body of Christ? *(Ephesians 2:13-22 will help you to formulate your answer.)*

Name some examples you've seen where peace was not treated as a priority worth pursuing above other, more self-gratifying desires.

PEACE IN RELATIONSHIPS

Earlier this week, we looked at Paul's illustration in Romans 14 concerning the eating of different types of food. Believers with Gentile backgrounds freely ate all things, while many of those with a Jewish background observed the ceremonial laws concerning food and felt convicted about eating foods that had been offered to idols. Paul's advice? Remain true to your own conviction in disputable matters such as these. *But*—he also offered a warning.

Turn to Romans 14:19-20 in your Bible, focusing on verse 20. What's the main principle Paul was addressing in this verse?

The work of God is so much more important than some trivial issue like what kind of food to eat (or what sorority to join, for goodness' sake). We're supposed to be pursuing peace and building one another up. Paul made this clear when he said, *"It is good not to eat meat or to drink wine, or to do anything by which your brother stumbles"* **(ROM. 14:21)**. Before exercising what we feel to be our freedoms, we need to be aware of how we're affecting others.

When the Holy Spirit opens your eyes to see a fellow believer who could be hurt by what you're about to do, this is generally His way of saying, "Not now!" It doesn't mean you've lost that freedom forever, but you're not to enjoy it in that moment. Pursuing peace and keeping a brother from stumbling outweighs personal freedoms.

Read James 3:14-18 in your Bible. James describes how we can discern wisdom from God. In verse 17 (in the margin), underline all of the descriptive words that are indicative of divine wisdom. Circle any that emphasize the principle of today's lesson.

> "But the wisdom from above is first pure, then peaceable, gentle, reasonable, full of mercy and good fruits, unwavering, without hypocrisy."
> JAMES 3:17

Now look at verse 14 (in the margin). Put an asterisk beside descriptive words that indicate "demonic" influence (v. 15) in our lives.

Use the space below to record any indicators you've felt or thought or observed regarding a specific area of your life where you are currently seeking to discern God's leading. Which comply with either *God's* wisdom or *demonic* wisdom, based on this passage?

GOD'S WISDOM	DEMONIC WISDOM

Now prayerfully consider what you've discovered in these verses and from answering these questions, as seen in the chart you just filled out. What do you sense God saying to you about His will for this situation now?

A STUMBLING BLOCK

My sister Chrystal (bless her heart) trips and falls more than anyone I know. As a family, we've had many laughs about her clumsiness. Whenever she's walking up or down stairs, especially when trying to carry or juggle anything in her arms, my mother and I hold our breath in fear. We do everything in our power to clear the path for her and prevent a catastrophe because we know she is prone to stumble.

> "But if you have bitter jealousy and selfish ambition in your heart, do not be arrogant and so lie against the truth."
> JAMES 3:14

As believers, our goal should be to clear the path in front of those who are prone to stumble, to protect them from a weakened conscience or a weakened commitment to the Lord. If we aren't careful, however, the enemy can take advantage of us, even in our trying to be considerate. He can transfer the pressure we feel to keep our fellow believers safe into an area of bondage for us, where we lose the ability to enjoy any freedoms because we're constantly worried about how they'll affect others. You know what I'm talking about? Have you ever felt that?

I can think of a dozen examples, easy, where this tension might come into play. Should other people's opinions be our principal guide in what we decide to do? Are they our substitute conscience? How worried should we be about what other people think? What if trying to be cautious with one group or person's feelings puts us at risk of disrupting our peace with someone else? Didn't Paul say, in another context, *"Am I trying to please people? If I were still trying to please people, I would not be a servant of Christ"* **(GAL. 1:10, NIV)**.

I've found the following to be good advice in managing this balancing act of freedom and forbearance. In order for someone to stumble—the warning Paul issued in the back half of Romans 14—the person must be *moving*, right? Generally moving *forward*. If you're sensing a check, a pause, or worrying that an action of yours might cause another to stumble, ask yourself if the person or people in mind are growing, maturing, and proactively seeking God. Those are the ones you need to be most concerned about. Other people—those who aren't even trying to grow, who aren't responding to what's obviously in front of their faces anyway—likely shouldn't factor into your decision. How can they stumble if they're not even moving?

○ YES ○ NO   Can you think of people in your life who fit the "moving forward" description?

If so, what's the Lord asking you to do in regard to them?

Being aware of how our actions will affect other believers is one way the Holy Spirit speaks to us. Why do you think the enemy might not want believers to recognize this element of God's personal communication with His people?

> Choose three of the following verses. Read each from your Bible, then record below how they speak to you regarding a current relationship in your life.
>
> • Psalm 34:14
> • Matthew 5:9
> • Mark 16:15
> • Romans 12:10
> • 1 Corinthians 10:33
> • Colossians 3:15

1.

2.

3.

God loves unity and always encourages us to pursue peace. When determining whether or not you're hearing God's voice, ask yourself:

• Will the message I'm hearing impede another's spiritual growth?

• Will it cause unnecessary conflict between myself and another believer?

If the answer to either of these questions is *yes*, pause and ask the Lord for clarity before moving forward. Better to delay your plans and seek the Lord's will from a pure heart, not wanting to do anything to shake another's faith or create unneeded distraction and turmoil that may require a lot of wasted time and explanation on the back end.

Pure, peaceable relationships are important to God. He will not lead us to hinder peace and unity in the body of Christ. This doesn't mean everyone will agree with what you're doing, but it does mean your decision will not cause another believer to stumble.

Take time to thank the Lord for the freedoms He's given you to enjoy, but also ask Him to make you sensitive to other believers. The Spirit's voice echoing within us will call us to peace with our brothers and sisters.

THE FIFTH DAY

Luke 24 provides a compelling end to this Gospel account. Luke alone included the story of two men (both presumably men, one named Cleopas) who were traveling a dusty road from Jerusalem to their hometown of Emmaus. They were possibly leaving Jerusalem after having participated in the Passover festivities. This year the gathering had been marked by great confusion and despair, of course, accented by the stunning crucifixion of Jesus of Nazareth, who'd claimed to be the promised Messiah of the Jews.

While the two made their way home, they were discussing these current events: Jesus' trial, His death, His burial. They were so engrossed in their conversation that when Jesus Himself joined their little caravan, they didn't even recognize He was the one they were discussing. *They were right there with Jesus and didn't even know it.*

Yet when their walk and conversation with this compelling stranger was over, they described to each other how they'd both felt while He was there.

Turn to Luke 24:32 and rewrite this verse in your own words.

Consider the *weight* that God's voice carries. Like an anchor securing a boat at sea, the words of God carry a weight that settles deep into your soul. His words are not flighty or fleeting. They resonate with authority—a deep, consistent burning that sears into your innermost being. Even when Jesus walked the earth, His words carried a unique influence that rang in the hearts of everyone who heard Him, stirring up amazement and conviction.

Our default in life is often to reason our way through, to survive on our facts-based assessments and our pros-and-cons lists. But when the Holy Spirit speaks, His words come with such sudden, passionate authority that they produce a holy amazement. The authority of His message will strike your inner man with such a blow that it will shake loose your old agenda and replace it with His new one.

> When the Holy Spirit speaks, His voice comes with a power that grips you.

It's Him.

You know it.

And like the men on the road to Emmaus, you look back and realize it.

As you close this week's lesson and prayerfully seal some of these truths that God has powerfully impressed on you, consider the *burning heart effect* and how it distinguishes the voice of God from all other voices in your life.

> "But if I say, 'I will not remember Him or speak anymore in His name,' then in my heart it becomes like a burning fire shut up in my bones; and I am weary of holding it in, and I cannot endure it."
> **JEREMIAH 20:9**

_____

_____

_____

_____

_____

_____

_____

_____

_____

_____

THE SOUND OF HIS VOICE

by Dr. Tony Evans

Scripture says the Holy Spirit is a Person. As such, He possesses certain qualities that differentiate Him from an inanimate object. We're told, for instance, that He possesses emotions, that we can *"grieve"* Him by our actions **(EPH. 4:30)**. We're told He has a *"mind"* **(ROM. 8:27)** and possesses an intellect. We're told He has a will (1 Cor. 12:11) and acts with purposeful intention. He is likened to a *"dove"* **(MATT. 3:16)**, implying that just as doves are gentle, sensitive birds that fly away quickly when approached or threatened, the Holy Spirit's voice can be easily muted if we are living in opposition to His holy character.

But how do we know when the voice we're hearing in our spirits is in fact His voice?

Christians today tend to operate between two extremes related to hearing the voice of the Spirit. They believe He either only speaks through Scripture (objectively) and does not speak subjectively at all in leading us to make day-to-day decisions. Or they believe the Spirit speaks only subjectively—His voice is somehow separate from the already written words of Scripture. You see this second mind-set especially (as Priscilla has described) when people become convinced of what they think God is telling them, even though Scripture clearly condemns what they are thinking, doing, and saying.

If you are hearing something that will lead you to glorify God, you are hearing the Holy Spirit. If what you're hearing forces you to reject the temptation to please yourself—if surrendering is a noticeable struggle—you are hearing from the Holy Spirit, and you need to push on. Walking in the Spirit will lead you to take steps in life that direct you in fulfilling His kingdom purposes. As

Paul said, *"The kingdom of God is not eating and drinking, but righteousness and peace and joy in the Holy Spirit"* **(ROM. 14:17)**.

In my own life, when I am in sync with the Holy Spirit, He floods my thoughts with ideas, directions, and warnings. I don't have to work at this; He just does it. I sense His release to move forward, or I sense His restriction to hold back, just as He did with those in the New Testament (Acts 11:12; 16:6-7). When I'm unsure, I look for confirmation, even as Gideon did with his two fleeces (Judg. 6:34-40). I see if it's confirmed by *"two or three witnesses"* **(1 TIM. 5:19)**. He wants to be heard, and He wants us to recognize the sound. So He takes pleasure in confirming His Word.

Far too many Christians are operating on autopilot. They get revved up on Sunday at church, then set their cruise control for the rest of the week—until they land in church the following Sunday. The Holy Spirit is real, and if we position ourselves spiritually, His voice will give us continued, personal direction. He speaks as plainly and as clearly as you and I allow His voice to be in our lives.

Reflective of His Heart

WEEK FOUR

"With _MY WHOLE HEART_ have I sought You, inquiring for
and of You and yearning for You; oh, let me not _WANDER_ or
step aside [either in ignorance or willfully] from Your commandments."

PSALM 119:10, AMPCE

To Hear God: _ReLAX Refocus_

"Whoever seeks God as a means toward desired ends will not find
God. The mighty God, the maker of heaven and earth, will not be
one of many treasures, not even the chief of all treasures. He will be
all in all or He will be nothing."[1] **A. W. TOZER**

To Hear God: _FOCUS_

It is _Our Responsibility_ to get to know God. It is His
responsibility to _Keep Us_ from wandering astray.

It is _God's Responsibility_ to cause you to hear and
recognize His voice.

Lead Me today to Help others PSM.

2 Corm 10:10 PS 46:10. EPH 4:30

PROV 3:5-6 Matt 6-9-13 Phil 3:15 2:13 Philippians 1:6

HE IS OUR PRIZE

"How happy we might be, if only we could find the Treasure, of which the Gospel tells us—all else would seem to us nothing. How infinite it is! The more one toils and searches in it, the greater are the riches that one finds."[2]

—BROTHER LAWRENCE

We have a family friend, Mrs. Holt, who's been part of our lives for many years, always offering kindness, friendship, encouragement, and the best Mexican food you've ever eaten in your life. When I graduated from the University of Houston, she surprised me with one of those beautiful, soft leather gift books, trimmed in gold foil, containing quotes about life and success. So lovely. So thoughtful. And I was so glad to have it. Only I didn't have time to read it. Busy with last-minute senior things, with ceremonies and festivities, with applications for graduate school, with packing up for my move back to Dallas, I put the book in a stack of other things and left it unused and unopened for a long time. Years actually.

Then one day—again, a number of years later—while going through some old boxes that had been stuffed away, I ran across this little book and smiled, thinking of Mrs. Holt's sweet face and her longtime generosity. And for the first time ever, I opened it.

A rectangular sliver of paper fluttered to the floor.

A check for $200.

Let me just say—two hundred dollars to a struggling new college graduate would have felt like twenty thousand. How I needed that kind of extra cash at the moment when she'd given it. All of that treasure, wasted! Because I never bothered to open the book.

I think you know that treasures of another kind come spilling out of your Bible every time you open it—when you *do* open it. But the greatest treasure that slips from its holy pages, the one you need above all others, is *God Himself.*

Listen, He is the prize. Not His direction, guidance, and clarity, not even His comfort, relief, and encouragement. Just Him. He is the One who encompasses all you are searching for.

MUTUAL AGREEMENT

When God speaks, His chief aim is to reveal Himself. He desires to make Himself known and lead you into a more intimate relationship with Him. If you overlook this main objective in search of more self-focused ambitions (even honorable ones), you will not be able to clearly discern His leading. The distorting filter of pride and self-importance will skew what you're hearing, mistaking the voice of your own ego for the voice of God. The clarity you desire comes from matching *your* chief aim in hearing Him with *His* chief aim in speaking to you. That's how you weed out the voice of strangers, as well as your own.

> According to John 16:14, what is the Holy Spirit's goal in revealing the Father's will to us? *Bring Glory*

The word glorify (or to bring glory) in John 16:14 means "to cause to have splendid greatness, clothe in splendor, glorify."[3]

PS 119:18

> Turn to John 17:4, preparing to notice the continuity between the Son's ambitions and the Spirit's ambitions. Jesus is speaking here. What does He specify as His chief aim?

One commentary explains the symmetry this way: "In 16:14-15, the Father is identified as the ultimate source of both the Son's and the Spirit's revelatory ministry to believers. There is continuity between the Son and the Spirit: just as the Son brought glory to the Father (7:18; 17:4), so the Spirit will bring glory to Jesus. There is also continuity between the Father and the Son and hence between Father/Spirit and Son/Spirit, with the persons of the Godhead collaborating in the task of divine self-disclosure."[4]

This is a fancy way of saying: the main business of the Trinity is to glorify one another. Back and forth, round and round. When that's your main business too, you're aligned with God's purposes and primed to hear His voice.

> Considering the Son's and the Spirit's chief aim, how does this help you distinguish His direction in your life from errant voices?

The Holy Spirit's main goals are to enhance the reputation of the Son and to shine a spotlight on the Father in such a way that Father and Son are honored and extolled. When He reveals the Father's thoughts to you, you will see this thread woven into what He is saying to you.

> In your own words, rewrite the Holy Spirit's intentions in communicating with you.

> If you are currently seeking to discern God's leading in a specific area and several options are in front of you, ask yourself: which option will enhance the reputation of God and highlight His character to me and to those in my sphere of influence? Record your thoughts below.

FOCUSED LISTENING

Let's be honest, our intentions in hearing God are not always pure. While well-intentioned, they can become misaligned in priority. It's easy to start seeking God's *direction* more than just seeking to know God Himself. If we aren't careful, we can wrongly venerate His *voice* over *Him*, making an idol out of one of His most intimate gifts to us.

This costly tradeoff is most clearly seen when we frantically try to solve our problems while neglecting the opportunity these problems provide us to simply *be* in His presence. When the frustration we feel from a lack of clarity about some area of our lives causes us to distance ourselves from church, from prayer, from God's Word—touch points where we can sit before God in worship and quietness—we can instantly tell that our priorities are out of order. We must constantly maintain the far superior privilege of knowing God over merely getting something from Him or implementing an action plan.

Reorient your focus. Don't bypass the relationship because you'd rather have answers to your questions. God wants to speak to you because He wants you to *know Him*. Knowing His direction is just a by-product. He wants to reveal truth about Himself to you because this knowledge will lay the firm path toward fulfilling His purpose for your life. Since this is *His* goal, making it *your* goal is key in differentiating His leading from the leading of others.

> Think carefully. What does your current desire to hear God's voice revolve mostly around?
> ○ Your desire to know what God wants you to do
> ○ Your desire to know where God wants you to go
> ○ Your desire to know God
>
> Record what God revealed about Himself in each of the passages below.
>
> Moses (Exodus 34:6-7)
>
>
>
> Malachi (Malachi 3:6-7a)

If you are in the process of waiting on God for clear direction, there is something about Himself that He is revealing to you in the meantime. Don't ignore it. Ask Him to reveal it.

This week, search the names of God online. Pick one or two of His names that mean the most to you, and share them with your group. His names signify His character.

Think back to the last time you were moved in a practical way by one of the characteristics of God in your own life, maybe as provider, healer, sustainer, or any number of divine attributes. Record the details of that here.

Is there any way your obedience fostered this experience? *Be prepared to discuss this with your small group.*

As we close today's lesson, I'm drawn to an often overlooked verse tucked within Psalm 103: *"He made known His ways to Moses, His acts to the sons of Israel"* **(V. 7).**

So short, sweet, and simple—yet, pregnant with meaning and insight. Do you notice the difference between what God did for Moses and what He did for Israel? Why don't you circle one and underline the other, just to highlight it on the page. Go ahead, I'll wait.

While the former *("His ways")* refers to God's manners, customs, and behaviors, the latter *("His acts")* points to His deeds. The first is far more intimate than the second. It's like the difference between a mother whose relationship with her child is based on cuddling with him on the sofa in the evenings, as opposed to being based mainly on the things she does for him (make his lunch, wash his clothes, take him to the doctor). Both aspects are good—"acts" and "ways"—but one is quite different from the other. And much richer.

In Israel's stubbornness, rebellion, and singular focus, God narrowed His interaction with them to merely showing them His wonders. Nice. But Moses enjoyed a more rewarding, far superior result—a deeper level of intimacy. God pulled back the veil in a more personal way with him, revealing His personality, His character, and His heart. And this was what Moses valued above all else. Listen to His request:

"Now if I have indeed found favor with you, please teach me your ways, and I will know you."
EXODUS 33:13, CSB

May the cry of Moses' heart be the cry of ours too!

When God chooses to speak to us, His Word will always in some way be designed to point us to Him and open up our understanding so that we can experience Him more fully. Without knowledge of the nature of God, obedience to Him becomes more difficult, if not impossible. The more you know and believe to be true about who God is and what He can do, the more willing you become to obey what He commands.

You can distinguish God's voice by asking these questions:

- Does what I am hearing show some truth about the character and nature of God as revealed in Scripture?

- Will obedience to this directive cause me to discover and experience an aspect of God's character?

When the enemy speaks to you, when your ego speaks to you, those voices will distort the character and Word of God. Anything that doesn't reflect the character of God or require you to more clearly see and experience Him is not a message from Him. Because this is His chief aim.

He alone is our prize.

HE LOVES YOU

"This message—I am someone God so loves—is a message we're likely to hear from God in contemplation. . . . God is so anxious to tell us this that the only time God is pictured in a hurry in Scripture is when the father ran down the trail to the prodigal son, 'threw his arms around him and kissed him.'"[5]

—JAN JOHNSON

I've spoken often of my college years in this study. Those impressionable, developmental years of life are so ripe for hearing God. Or for—*not* hearing God.

My college years took me from the sheltered life of my Christian family to another world. All at the same time, I was both overwhelmed and excited by the lifestyle before me. However, I soon found myself living contrary to what I knew would please the Lord. As a result, I struggled with quite a bit of guilt in the years that followed. No matter what I accomplished in life or how far I removed myself from the choices I had made, a nagging voice in my head kept pouring on the guilt. I lost sleep, struggled to maintain health in new relationships, and felt haunted by a sense of shame.

Ever been there? Know those feelings?

As I continued struggling to get free from these dead weights on my heart and mind, in my quiet time one day, I ran across a couple of verses that seemed to jump up off the page and burrow into the depths of my soul.

 "Now this is what the LORD says—the one who created you, Jacob, and the one who formed you, Israel—'Do not fear, for I have redeemed you; I have called you by your name; you are mine.'"
ISAIAH 43:1, CSB

> "I sweep away your transgressions for my own sake
> and remember your sins no more."
> **ISAIAH 43:25, CSB**

Tears welled in my eyes as I recognized God's personal word to me.
*I have redeemed you. You are Mine. I sweep away your transgressions.
I remember your sins no more. Ahh!* It was the voice of God telling me
He had delivered me from the guilt of my past by showering me with
grace and moving me toward the promise of tomorrow. That constant
sense of condemnation and burdensome cloak of guilt I'd been
wrestling to shrug off—it couldn't be coming from God since it was
incongruent with His character. All the critical and ominous sentiments
I'd been believing had left me devoid of grace and hope, thinking
they summed up His opinion of me and His outlook for me. But, they
didn't match how He described Himself in these verses.

So if it wasn't *Him*, it must have been—

Yes, after reading those verses a few more times, I began to clearly recognize the fingerprints of the enemy in what I'd been previously hearing.
He'd been using my past against me—to keep me from being able to
flourish, walk in abundance, and experience victory as a daughter of
God. Wouldn't that be just like him? And so unlike my Father?

Fill in the blanks below by looking back at one of the
previous paragraphs.

God's voice seeks to deliver me from the guilt of ___MY___
___PAST___ by showering me with [~~LOVE~~] __GRACE__ and
moving me toward the promise of __~~tomorrow~~__.
              __TOMORROW__

Yesterday's lesson is a building block for today's theme. Look back at
what we learned to be the Holy Spirit's chief aim, and write it in the
oval below.

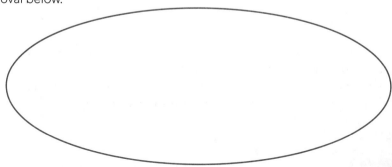

*Condemnation is
the work of the
enemy. It means to
consider something
worthy of punish-
ment. Conviction is
the work of the Holy
Spirit. It means to
bring something to
light in order
to correct it.*

Since this is the Holy Spirit's intention (or goal), we know that one of the distinguishing characteristics which will identify His voice is that it will highlight His great, never-ending love for us.

Love. It's not merely something God exhibits; love is a trait that is innate to His being. *"God is love"* (**1 JOHN 4:8**). What water is to an ice cube, love is to God. God and love aren't merely intertwined. They are one and the same. There is no love without God, and no God without love. If what you are hearing is not punctuated by love (and by one or more of its companions, such as hope, grace, or mercy), you're not hearing God. Even when He is disciplining and correcting you, He is still operating from His foundational character of love. Love is who He is. It's what His voice continually invites us all to experience.

> Look up 1 Corinthians 13:4-8. In the left-hand column of the chart below (A), write words and phrases that describe God's love. In the right-hand column (B), write antonyms that describe the voice of the enemy.

LIST A	LIST B

> In an area of your life where you're seeking to discern God's leading, does what you're hearing align more with the words in list A or list B?

Listen clearly: God does point out our sin. And that may not always sound *loving* to us. But He doesn't *convict* of sin for the purpose of *condemning* us. His purpose in lovingly revealing our sin is only to lead us to acknowledge it and confess it so He can change us. The

Romans 5:10

enemy's voice brings condemnation. You will know condemnation because it's accompanied by guilt that offers no clear means of relief. On the other hand, the Holy Spirit brings conviction that always provides a road map out and away from a specific sin. His aim is always to lovingly steer us in the direction of His grace and toward intimacy with the Father.

Romans 5:10 brings clarity to this point. Look it up in your Bible. A key word appears twice in this verse. Identify it, and write it below. *RECONCILED*

When the Father sent His Son to take your place on Calvary, He didn't just do it for the singular purpose of forgiving you. While forgiveness is certainly one of the glorious ramifications of the cross, there's something more. His gift was also designed to *reconcile* you to the Father. (That's the word I was looking for.) The word *reconcile* paints a picture of two people making peace and amends after a hearty quarrel. Reconciliation is the beautiful love story by which the divide of sin between you and God is eternally bridged. This friendship with God is the promise of the gospel! And, listen to me, it is also the ongoing promise of His friendship with us.

That's why, when He speaks to you, His words will carry this continued hope of intimacy, friendship, and reconciled relationship.

In your own words, what is the difference between condemnation and conviction?

If you now recognize something you've been hearing to be the condemning voice of the enemy, stop right now and tell God in prayer that you now recognize these words are not from Him. As you do, cross through any of the words in the previous chart (p. 112) that describe what you've been hearing. Let this symbolize your decision to no longer allow these thoughts to govern your thinking.

NO CONDEMNATION

In John 8, a group of Pharisees brought a woman caught in adultery into the temple. They stood her in front of Jesus. Then, these men revealed her sin, exposing her as a lawbreaker and embarrassing her before the crowd—all in an attempt, the Bible says, *"to trap [Jesus], in order that they might have evidence to accuse him"* **(V. 6, CSB)**.

You've heard this story enough times to know what Jesus did next. He said to her accusers, *"He who is without sin among you, let him be the first to throw a stone at her"* **(V. 7)**. This meant He was the only person qualified to condemn her. And He didn't throw the stone.

Did you hear that? *He did not throw the stone!*

Hallelujah! God alone has the right to condemn us, yet He has chosen not to throw stones. Then or now. He bestows grace and love despite what we have done because His very nature is love. This is what distinguishes His voice from any other.

Whenever I feel the pain of "stones" thrown at me, I quickly realize they didn't come from my Lord. When I have missed having my quiet time, for instance, and begin to feel guilty, I recognize this guilt isn't the Lord scolding me into compliance. He doesn't want me to come to Him out of guilt but out of love and affection. I know He is wooing me when I feel a compelling *conviction*, not a berating *condemnation*, that tenderly urges me to respond to His love.

> In what areas do you tend to operate out of guilt rather than love?

> Read John 8:10-11 in the margin and underline Jesus' two main messages to the woman.

One by one, the Pharisees realized they wouldn't be able to meet Jesus' qualifications for condemning this woman, so they left. Then Jesus spoke. He didn't dismiss her sin or make excuses for it; He just didn't condemn her for it.

"Jesus said to her, 'Woman, where are they? Did no one condemn you?' She said, 'No one, Lord.' And Jesus said, 'I do not condemn you, either. Go. From now on sin no more.'"

JOHN 8:10-11

This is what His voice will say to you as well. Even in pointing out your sin, He will offer grace so you can continue on in righteousness. He doesn't bring up the past without pointing toward the future.

When God speaks to us, His words will not heap judgment on us. He reveals our sins to lead us to repentance, buffering this acknowledgment of our failure with the hope of His grace, love, and another chance. *Go—and sin no more—*because He has already undergone the punishment for our sin once and for all on the cross.

Describe how God's voice brought both conviction and encouragement in the following examples.

	CONVICTION	ENCOURAGEMENT
2 Chronicles 7:13-14		
Isaiah 1:16-18		
Ezekiel 18:30-32		

Condemnation offers only guilt and judgment as it points out the problem; the soothing conviction of God offers a solution. You will know God's voice because it will bring encouragement along with conviction.

Be encouraged today. Be hopeful. This is what a loving Father would say to you, His beloved child.

"The purpose of the voice of condemnation is to push you away from His presence—that which is the very source of your victory. The purpose of the voice of conviction is to press you into the face of Christ."[6]
BOB SORGE

NOTHING BUT THE TRUTH

The action/adventure film *Inception* takes moviegoers on a wild ride into the various realms of people's dreams, where at ever deeper levels the lines between fact and fiction become harder to distinguish. Even when the happenings in the film are bizarre and unpredictable, the dream states seem remarkably lifelike to the characters inside them.

That's why, after years of delving inside his own dreams and the dreams of others, the lead character increasingly struggles to ascertain his whereabouts. He's been fooled many times. His senses have been deceived. So he's established the habit of carrying an item in his pocket—a spinning top—to help him determine whether he is currently in reality or still inside a dream. When he spins that top into motion on a flat surface, he knows—if he's in the real world—it will eventually succumb to the pull of gravity and fall over. If he's not, the top will continue in a perpetual spin. Instead of basing his next move on his own feelings and perceptions, he's learned the importance of an objective standard. It's the only thing that helps him know—*the truth*.

Listen to me: Your feelings, past experiences, and personal perceptions cannot be wholly trusted. If you depend on them, you'll likely be deceived by the enemy. He is a master illusionist. To keep from being fooled, you must possess an objective standard outside of yourself so he can't keep pulling the wool over your eyes. *God's Word is that objective standard.* It is the unchanging, uncompromising truth that will help you achieve clarity to know where you really are and what is really happening around you.

> Circle the three human attributes from the first sentence of the previous paragraph. Below, record the one to which you usually give the most credence in your own decision-making.

Look up the familiar verse John 14:6, and fill in the blank below. *(It's nearly identical in most all Bible translations.)*

"I am the way, and the _____, and the life; no one comes to the Father but through Me."

Consider this divine attribute (of *truth*) in relation to the personal one you just wrote down about yourself. How have you seen these two collide and contradict?

Throughout nearly every week of this study, we've circled back around to the centrality of the Bible in correctly hearing God. It is not only the chief means through which God speaks, but it's also the boundary into which everything else will fall.

But today I want you to see *why* you can depend on the Word and *how* it can help you distinguish God's voice from those of imposters. The Word reflects a central character trait of God. *Truth* is His nature. *"Let God be found true, though every man be found a liar"* **(ROM. 3:4)**. He cannot and will not ever lie because no deception is found in His character. The convictions and leadings we receive from Him will never contain a tinge of duplicity or dishonesty. He will never contradict His character or His purposes as revealed in His written Word. He will never lead you into sin, never steer you outside of His will, and never encourage you to cover up your offenses.

The facet of God's character that is also the calling card of His communication to you is _____.

Look at John 16:13 in the margin. Read it carefully and underline this characteristic wherever it appears or is implied.

According to this verse, what causes the Holy Spirit to reveal truth to people?

> "When He, the Spirit of truth, comes, He will guide you into all the truth; for He will not speak on His own initiative, but whatever He hears, He will speak; and He will disclose to you what is to come."
>
> **JOHN 16:13**

God's Spirit doesn't speak on His own initiative. He is not a renegade agent trying to accomplish a different agenda or objective apart from God the Father and God the Son. Every message the Spirit delivers comes straight from the God of truth. Only the Holy Spirit has direct access to the Father's thoughts. (See 1 Cor. 2:10.) He lives in you and desires to share these revelations with those who will listen.

When the Spirit of God is truly the One speaking to you, you'll know it because He will only speak the truth, the whole truth, and nothing but the truth.

LIES, LIES, AND MORE LIES

Jordyn is a successful, beautiful woman, one of the kindest, most considerate people I've ever known. She believes in Jesus and has truly desired to honor Him throughout her life. To hear her tell it, this is why she spent much of her life suppressing her attraction to other women, a situation that's left her feeling guilty, condemned, judged, and increasingly embittered, to the point of being estranged from the church. At age 45, she's decided the loneliness she feels cannot be God's will for her. Since these same-sex attractions have only solidified until they feel more and more natural, she's concluded this must be God's way of condoning her decision to simply embrace "who she is." She feels good about it now. Based on certain Scriptures she's carefully selected (and taken out of context), she says she's been affirmed that pursuing this path is indeed God's will for her life.

But could this be *true*? I know this woman. I know of her faith and belief in Christ. If the Holy Spirit truly indwells her, how she could be so off-base about God's voice?

We've all been in this position at one time or another. Different circumstances, same dilemma. We've been certain about an action we planned to take, a decision we needed to make. We've based it on deep-rooted emotional responses or solid rationalizations. To us, we thought we were doing the right thing.

But as usual, hindsight tells us differently. The enemy's approach is so cryptic and clever that we rarely know he's taking advantage of us in the moment. He is able to mirror God's voice and will so closely that, without a reliable sounding board to evaluate and measure it, we are likely to be led astray.

> According to the following verses, what are some of the actions and attributes that describe the enemy?

Matthew 4:1

John 8:44

Revelation 12:10

How are these satanic methods antagonistic toward truth?

In order to hear God's voice—in order to discern it from the enemy's lies, temptations, and accusations—we must pause, step back, and return to the objective standard of God's Word. Like the character in *Inception*, we must spin the top. We must take that voice for a spin through the Scripture. Not just picking and choosing where we visit but going anywhere He takes us. If it's God speaking, what He's saying will align with biblical truth. And if it's not, it won't—or at least not completely.

Jordyn might have felt affirmed by her own desires and even cultural norms to make the decisions she had chosen, but she wasn't being led by the Holy Spirit. What she heard clearly misrepresented the standards set by God in His Word.

Look at some of these common examples. Choose two of the statements below (or add your own) and describe why each misrepresents God's Truth. Feel free to use the margin if you need it. Add any Scripture you know that validates your response. I've helped you out on a few of them. *Be prepared to discuss this with your small group and add to the list.*

- I don't need to be part of a local church (Heb. 10:24-25).

- I don't like the decision my husband is making. I refuse to follow him in this matter (Eph. 5:22-23).

- I'm a Christian, but I feel unworthy. I know God doesn't hear me when I pray (Mic. 7:7; Heb. 10:22).

- I don't make enough money to tithe right now. God understands (Mal. 3:8-10).

-

-

What are some other common scenarios in which you've seen others (or yourself) rely on feelings and rationalizations above God's Truth?

All of the excuses in this activity sound rational, don't they? I mean, seriously, should tithing be required of me when money is running short? Should submitting to God-given leadership still apply when my preference is contrary to my husband's? If I don't feel it or if it doesn't make sense, then—*to me*, it isn't true. I'm right. I'm justified.

This is precisely how the enemy sneaks in, disguised and cloaked in rationalizations and misrepresentations which in the moment seem easier, better, and far more convenient.

STANDING FIRM

In the first week of our Bible study, I mentioned how impactful Ephesians 6:10-20 has been in my life. In this passage, Paul articulates a vivid, step-by-step plan of action for spiritual victory by correlating different spiritual virtues such as righteousness, peace, and faith to different pieces of a soldier's armor.

One of the simplest, yet most impactful, things I discovered was that the first piece of armor a soldier put on was a belt (more like a girdle) that he would wear under the rest of his uniform. It was the central piece—a requirement for everything else to hang and hinge properly. Paul correlates this first piece of armor to truth in the believer's life. *"Stand, therefore, with truth like a belt around your waist"* **(V. 14, CSB)**.

Since the enemy is a master deceiver, hearing God accurately requires a commitment to gird ourselves in truth, to situate it at our core, and to use it as the compass for the entirety of our lives. Otherwise, the enemy's illusions are too crafty. If we *"lean on [our] own understanding"* instead of acknowledging God *"in all [our] ways"* **(PROV. 3:5-6)**, we don't stand a chance against the enemy's schemes.

> "The sum of Your word is truth, and every one of Your righteous ordinances is everlasting."
> **PSALM 119:160**

God's standard of truth may differ from the standard of your family, denomination, or culture. As you can imagine, the process of unraveling and retraining our thinking to align with truth can be arduous and take time. But just because we feel comfortable doing something doesn't make it right. We must filter it through the truth of God and bring our behavior and attitudes into alignment with that truth. *His Word is truth.* And when His Spirit speaks, He will only speak truth.

> Have you pledged personal allegiance to the Bible's precepts as the guiding factor of your life?

Hearing it, reading it, even memorizing it is not enough. I hope you do all these things, of course. But you must do something more. You must humble yourself underneath its authority.

> "Sanctify them in the truth; Your word is truth."
> **JOHN 17:17**

The enemy is hoping you'll think you are smart enough, perceptive enough, savvy enough, experienced enough that you can trust yourself to recognize God's fingerprints and voice quality. He knows that any one of us who gets too big for our spiritual britches and no longer pledges full allegiance to the unchanging standards of God's Word can be carried away by his craftiness.

What we need is the truth. And in God and His Word, that's exactly what we get.

PEACE PATROL

As a young preacher in Dallas, my father had an internal peace about a direction the Lord had given him for ministry. He believed God wanted his small church to own not only the building where they met but the whole *street*—giving them enough space to build other buildings that could serve the needs of the entire community.

Only one problem. Well, lots of problems with a plan this large, but the most obvious, pressing problem was that they didn't have any money to buy the land. When there's not enough money to fund a major endeavor, people tend not to hop on board the dream train.

Still, God's peace ruled in Tony Evans's heart. And while many people, both inside and outside the congregation, were saying this proposal was impossible, he moved forward in obedience, expecting to see God's supernatural activity as a result.

> "Peace I leave with you; my peace I give to you. Not as the world gives do I give to you. Let not your hearts be troubled, neither let them be afraid."
> JOHN 14:27, ESV

Today, Oak Cliff Bible Fellowship does indeed own the entire street on which it sits, as well as many of the businesses that line its storefronts. This innovative arrangement has given the church a remarkable platform to reach people with the gospel throughout the years by way of nontraditional yet highly effective means—all because peace ruled in my father's heart, confirming a divinely orchestrated purpose that even the strongest naysayers and difficulties couldn't destroy.

A strong and consistent sense of internal peace can clue you into the sound of God's voice.

RULES OF THE ROAD

Before Jesus died, He offered comforting words to His disciples. He explained that He was leaving His peace with them, to care and provide for them after He was gone. His peace would serve as an internal mechanism by which they could discern God's voice.

God's _____ serves as an internal mechanism by which I can discern _____ _____.

Name some differences between the peace Jesus gives and the so-called peace that comes from the world, from other sources.

Peace is a gift that accompanies our salvation. *"Having been justified by faith, we have peace with God through our Lord Jesus Christ"* **(ROM. 5:1)**. It is also a fraternal twin of *grace* (another beautiful word in our spiritual vocabulary). They're frequently seen together in Scripture as a prayerful blessing of God's favor, spoken between believers. *"Grace to you and peace from God our Father and the Lord Jesus Christ"* **(PHIL. 1:2)**.

Peace is not only an element of His character, but it is also evidence of His presence.

The real, underlying reason why we're given peace to enjoy as a fringe benefit of our redemption and as a fruit of the Spirit (see Gal. 5:22) is because peace is just naturally generated by the *"God of peace"* **(ROM. 15:33)**. Peace (like *love*, like *truth*) is another of God's identifying characteristics and is, therefore, an identifying marker that can direct our antenna in the direction of the Spirit's voice. Peace plays a vital role in hearing God.

In our study last week, we saw how we can expect His voice to place a priority on pursuing peace among brothers and sisters in Christ. That's true. But God's peace has an *internal* purpose in addition to its external one. When He speaks to you, His Word will be accompanied by a peaceful assurance in your heart. Despite the challenges ahead of you or the naysayers around you, His voice will cause you to feel anchored by a solid sense of calm about the task He is sending you to perform.

"Let the peace of Christ, to which you were also called in one body, rule your hearts."
COLOSSIANS 3:15, CSB

Colossians 3:15 (see the margin) helps us to better understand the role peace plays in discerning God's leading. What does this verse say the peace of God is supposed to do in your heart?

In the New Testament city of Colossae, believers struggled with a number of temptations and decisions. In regard to these issues, Paul told them to let peace be the guiding, determining factor in their choices. The Greek word that is translated *rule* in our English Bible—to *rule* in their hearts—is significant. It means to act as a judge or umpire.[7]

How would you describe the role of a modern-day judge in a court of law or an umpire on a field of play?

The peace of God serves as an umpire in our souls. It calls the play. When something is "out," you'll sense an uneasy lack of peace. When something is "safe" and "in bounds," it will promote a sense of peace internally that leaves you feeling more secure in God's direction.

I mentioned the analogy of a traffic light in the video teaching for Session Two of our study. Now, I want you to put yourself in the driver's seat and test drive the illustration. Have you ever sat at an intersection where the lights weren't working, perhaps flashing a blinking red or yellow? How did you feel about inching out into the oncoming traffic, knowing the signal above you was indicating caution and careful awareness? If that same light were to turn a steady green, you'd feel confident in following it straight through to the other side. Right? You'd have *peace* about it.

The "red light" of conviction = Stop

The "yellow light" of dis-ease = Wait

The "green light" of peace = Go

In regard to a specific personal issue you're facing, in which you want to discern God's direction right now, which of the three indicators in the margin would you use to describe the current feeling in your heart?

Recall a time when you moved forward without a completely green light. What were the results?

PRACTICING PEACE

When peace reigns in a matter you're dealing with—when you feel a deep inner assurance and permission—pay close attention to what you're hearing and sensing. You may be wrestling with a decision about a job offer in another city or an employee you need to hire. Maybe you're trying to decide which contractor to use for some remodeling work on your house or how to approach a friend who seems to be straying into sin. Perhaps it's a complete career change toward something you've never felt released to actively pursue. Maybe it's a ministry position at church that you admit you feel unqualified for, but you think God might be leading you to accept. Or a major purchase you've been studying and researching. It could be any number of things. In any case, carefully and prayerfully weigh your options in light of that inner peace. If there's restlessness and conviction—*wait*. But if there's a steady, solid, gripping settledness deep within, despite whatever difficulties you may face—*proceed*.

I realize, of course, sometimes peace may fluctuate. Here today, gone tomorrow—here right now, gone in ten minutes. I realize, too, that the *feeling* of peace is sometimes not *real* peace, and sometimes feelings of distress can be false readings as well. But *trust Him*—because letting peace "rule" is His biblical instruction to you.

Is your heart right? Do you truly want to know His will? As far as you're aware, are you obeying Him in all areas? No unconfessed sin? No relationships you're stirring up? No holdouts of unforgiveness?

Then trust His peace. Look for it. Practice depending on it.

It's how He speaks.

> Turn to John 20, a passage that describes events that occurred in the days following Jesus' resurrection. What did He offer the disciples in verse 19 to calm their edgy nerves at this time of roller coaster emotions?

What about in verse 21?

What did Jesus do next (in verse 22) to reinforce the peace He wanted them to experience?

Your own heart, left to itself, might quiver and hesitate and ultimately fail, but the Spirit's peace soothes and strengthens you. He keeps returning you to a sense of confidence, a new-every-morning assurance that He is working everything together, that you can accomplish the task He's sending you out to perform, even if many (most?) other indicators are waving red flags and conspiring to discourage you. Even if it scares you, the God of peace is speaking. He's converting the normal formulas you consult to determine your next steps, and He's causing them to add up to a peaceful resolution.

As believers, of course, we can never lose the God-given peace of our eternal salvation. Hallelujah! But we know, everyday life and the foreboding concerns of our modern age are not often conducive to maintaining a steady stream of peace. Yet when the Spirit is speaking, He causes you to experience peace inside. Not dreamy, wistful, holding-hands-in-a-circle peace but a peace that is strong, intense, palpable, real.

If you're wandering *even by accident* out of the path He's set for you, His peace will not rule. If you're moving forward prematurely, ahead of His timing, His peace will not rule. But when He is truly speaking to you on a particular matter, peace will settle deeply within your heart. *Wait for His peace to rule!*

When you feel a contest of wills ensuing in your heart—an uneasiness that makes you think twice about something—tune in to His peace signal. Take seriously what you're sensing. He is steering you to safety. And you can trust Him every single time.

Sometimes the need to seek out many people's opinions is an indicator that peace is simply not ruling. That's the time to practice the first of the Five Ms—look for the MESSAGE of the Spirit.

THE FIFTH DAY

Matthew had been married for five years when his relationship with his wife began to struggle. He took his concerns to the Lord and asked Him for help—asking God to show him what to do, how to handle this intense, confusing, upsetting time of his young life.

Perhaps what Matthew really wanted—what many of us have often wanted when praying for help—is for God to step in and change his wife's heart, to convict her of the ways she was misunderstanding him, misjudging him, mistreating him, creating all this turmoil and not seeing her own part in it. But while Matthew was spending time in prayer and in the Scripture, certain verses began to grip his heart, settling with authority into the depths of his being. A number of these verses reminded him of the sacrifice Christ had made for his salvation, of the unconditional love God had shown him, of His steadfast, forgiving, undying faithfulness through every season of Matthew's life.

The Spirit was speaking—directing this man to begin seeing his wife through the Lord's eyes, to start thinking and acting toward her with the compassionate patience that God had extended to Matthew—to put God's character traits into practice.

> "For the ways of the LORD are right, and the righteous will walk in them."
> HOSEA 14:9

Emerging from this time with the Lord, he noticed a stark change. His wife was the same, his marriage was the same, his various problems at home were the same—but, Matthew was surprisingly different. God's voice, reflecting God's character, had led him to see his wife through a whole new lens. Many dozens of years later, the love and devotion of this couple still testify to the redeeming, transformative power of God's Word.

List some of God's character traits we've studied this week. What others come to mind as you think about what you know of Him?

Recall a time when God's Word, revealing God's character, produced a change in your life. What were some of the immediate impacts? What could easily have happened if you hadn't heard and responded to His voice?

As you wrap up this vital week of lessons, refer back to the "Five Ms of Correctly Hearing God" that were introduced on page 55. Focus especially on the need for searching out *"the MODEL of Scripture."* As you think about what you've sensed the Lord saying to you since you embarked on this study, on this journey, how much of it stands in complete conformity with what you know to be true of His character? How does the Scripture back it up and confirm it? Even in some of the other areas listed in the Five Ms—prayer, wise counsel, ongoing confirmation—how does what you're hearing resonate with certain traits of God's nature, providing you with threads you can follow directly to His heart?

This is your day to spend however you want. I pray it's a really special one—hearing from God.

_____

_____

_____

_____

_____

_____

_____

_____

_____

_____

_____

_____

_____

THE IMPORTANCE OF INTIMACY

by Dr. Tony Evans

My wife, Lois, and I have been married for more than forty-seven years. Over that period of time, we have gotten to know each other pretty well, even though (as in all marriages), we are still in the discovery process. Because of our years together, we find ourselves often saying the same thing at the same time or even thinking the same thing simultaneously. When we need to make a decision about something, but we're not physically in the same place to talk it over, we can still hear each other inaudibly in our heads, typically voicing the same response as if we were both present. Knowledge of a person enables you to hear them speak even when their audible voice cannot be heard.

God's voice seems so faint to many Christians because they want the equivalent of a dating relationship with Him. But, He is looking for marriage. A holy union. Oneness. He wants us to prioritize our relationship with Him above all else. This is why He told the church at Ephesus, *"I have this against you, that you have left your first love"* **(REV. 2:4)**. He said unless they again prioritized their relationship with Him, He would remove Himself from their midst. Conversely, He promises to develop an intimate relationship with believers who seek to draw near to Him. He desires a committed relationship, which will lead to receiving the knowledge of His will—knowledge that comes from time spent together in prayer and meditation around His Word.

In 1 Chronicles 14:8-17, God gave David instructions on how to successfully fight a battle against the Philistines. David sought the Lord in prayer, and God gave him a clear strategy to follow, resulting in defeat of the enemy. But soon, the problem reappeared. The Philistines reassembled to launch another raid. When David sought the Lord in prayer this time, God gave him a different course of action to follow, resulting in defeat of the enemy a second time. Because David was in such close contact with God, he could hear Him give two totally different directives about the same concern. Without such an intimate relationship, we work off assumptions rather than fresh illumination from God.

When I watch the national weather report on television, I hear a general overview of weather conditions across the country. When I listen to the weather on my local stations, however, I hear details about where I live. God doesn't want us only receiving big-picture communication from Him but also specific guidance for our own lives—where we live. Having an up-close relationship with Him is essential to creating the climate for this dynamic to happen. We must continually foster this relationship through a surrendered life of worship and a transformed heart and mind, seeking to obey. When we do this, God promises we will know *"what the will of God is, that which is good and acceptable and perfect"* **(ROM. 12:2)**.

Revealing of His Plans

WEEK FIVE

Principle #1—God _____ _____ _____ in the desert.

Bushes don't burn in _____. They burn in deserts.

"God whispers to us in our pleasures, speaks in our conscience, but shouts in our pain."[1] **C. S. LEWIS**

_____ _____ to seeing God's plan while in the desert is to take your attention off of the _____ and place them on God's presence in the circumstances.

Principle #2—God _____ _____ for His purposes in the desert.

He's giving you the _____, the substance, the _____, the foundational work that will be necessary for Him to accomplish His work through you.

Principle #3—God _____ your _____ in the desert.

ON PURPOSE

"Nothing pleases God more than when we ask for what He wants to give. When we spend time with Him and allow His priorities, passions, and purposes to motivate us, we will ask for the things that are closest to His heart."[2]

—BRUCE WILKINSON

You may or may not know the name Arthur Blessitt. If not, you're likely to have heard of what he's best known *for*. In the 1960s, he opened a little coffee shop in Hollywood, California, and constructed a large wooden cross which he nailed to the wall in his new establishment. Soon, however, he felt compelled to take the cross down and carry it out into the streets. Eventually he would carry it across the country and around the world. On foot.[3]

I'm not joking.

On Christmas Day 1969, he began his first walk.[4] And since then, he's literally "carried his cross" into every sovereign nation on the planet, including many island groups and other land masses, covering all seven continents—more than 42,000 miles at last counting.[5] He is listed in the *Guinness Book of World Records* for the "Longest Ongoing Pilgrimage."[6]

It's been a unique undertaking, to say the least. And though it's easy for critics to question whether or not Blessitt heard from God in launching out on such an unusual ministry (it's not our place to judge), you've got to love this quote he made about his wooden cross, many years after he began his journey. "If I knew I was going to have to carry it around the world, I wouldn't have made it so big."[7]

Ahh, yes, I can relate to his sentiment. Can't you?

If we could have it our way, following God wouldn't require as much effort and strain as it sometimes does. Our manicured nails wouldn't need to get chipped or dirtied, our spiritual muscles wouldn't need to be stretched or strengthened, our own dreams and ambitions wouldn't need to be submitted. We could serve Him with little resistance. The cross we'd construct for ourselves to carry would be small, pocket-sized, easily ignored, and conveniently stowed.

And yet God's plans are frequently different from our own. His plans do not placate our low standards or personal expectations. His agenda far exceeds our tiny, myopic, narrow perspectives, requiring things of us that His Spirit must strengthen us to accomplish. Carrying the cross He gives us requires a grit and tenacity we may not have intended to exercise.

Therefore, accurately distinguishing God's voice requires a realignment of our hearts in humility and submission. We must yield our personally advantageous, self-made crosses, setting them aside altogether. Otherwise, by clinging to our demands for ease or pleasure, we'll miss many divinely ordained opportunities, and we'll muffle our ability to hear the voice of God.

> Look up the following references, and ask the Lord to speak to you through them. What do these verses say about God's plans? Record any ways in which these sentiments are meaningful to you personally.
>
> Psalm 81:13-14
>
>
>
> Ephesians 1:4
>
>
>
> Ephesians 2:10

As we jump into this week of study, ask yourself: Do I *really* desire to hear the Father's purposes for me and submit to His plans, or do I mainly desire to pursue my own purposes, hoping for His blessing on them? Your response will help clear away the internal noise that keeps you from accurately discerning God's leading in your life.

Search your heart. Prayerfully and authentically choose which you desire most:
🕭 To know God's plans and adjust my life to fit with them
○ To proceed with my plans and hope God will bless them

Last week, we learned about funneling what we hear from the Holy Spirit through the prism of God's *character*, as revealed in His Word. But we must also funnel it through God's *purposes*. Just as He will never speak a word to us that will contradict His character, He will also never say anything that is outside of His sovereignly designed plans for our lives or not in line with His kingdom agenda.

BLUEPRINTS

Ever since my husband and I were married, we've been saving our pennies to build a house someday. For the last couple of years, we've been working with an architect to design the floor plan, admittedly taking our sweet little old time on this first stage—crafting the blueprint.

We were advised early on in the process that spending time with the architect on the front end is crucial—because every subcontractor who will eventually pour the foundation, lay brick and mortar, run electrical cable, and put in the trim work will be following the detailed plans drawn on these original construction documents. These laborers may not immediately see how their individual contributions fit into the rest of the design, but the fact that they're following the established guidelines of the master plan will ensure that the whole house looks, feels, and functions the way it's supposed to, even as they bring their individual expertise and flair to the project.

God has a plan—an overarching blueprint for the construction of our lives, a compilation of specs and details that accomplish His purposes. The whole design is already in place. We can try, of course, to draft a different one. We can act as though we're a better judge of how our

> "When we seek to promote our-selves or when we ask God to make our plans successful, we will not always hear what we want to hear in response. However, when we ask him for guid-ance according to what is on *his* heart and when we ask how we can adjust our lives to *his* plans, the Bible says we will hear him clearly."[8]
>
> **HENRY & RICHARD BLACKABY**

DISCERNING
THE VOICE
OF GOD

136

lives should work and what they should look like. But God has thought of everything. Can you just trust Him in that? The Architect of your life knows exactly what He is doing. He knows what you love and what delights you the most, based on how He's created you, and He has incorporated all these things into a plan that best enables you to do what He wants done, even as you express your individuality—even if you can't see how some of the details fit together in the overall design.

Turn to Genesis 6:13-16. How would you describe God's instructions to Noah when constructing the ark?
○ General
○ Detailed
○ Ambivalent

List any observations from this passage that support your answer.

Is there an area of your life where you're concerned God will not disclose to you the details of His plan? How is trusting God's blueprint particularly difficult for you right now, given the lack of specifics you may have received?

For further study, encourage yourself with these extended biblical accounts:

• Gideon's army
  (Judg. 7:2-18)

• The construction of the tabernacle
  (Ex. 25–30)*

  * Note the attention to detail and God's intention for revealing it.

I admit, I've often plowed ahead with my own purposes, hoping God would give them His seal of approval. When He didn't, I was frustrated and disappointed, sometimes questioning His love for me and His concern for my well-being. But the truth is, I was trying to bend His will to mine, rather than mine to His. Why should I expect Him to encourage me in it or equip me for its success?

Your loving Father has a specific agenda for your career, ministry, finances, and family—a good and satisfying plan that graciously involves you in the vast purposes of His kingdom. And these plans—God's plans—will be more satisfying and fulfilling than any self-styled blueprints you could dream up and try to build on.

Check out 1 Kings 12:25-33 and its eye-opening example of someone who does *not* align himself with God's plan. Record five observations that you glean from this passage.

1.

2.

3.

4.

5.

Look at verse 28 in the margin. Underline the adjective that Jeroboam used in describing worship in Jerusalem.

King Jeroboam wanted a small, comfortable, easy-to-carry cross for the people to bear. Good public relations? Yes. Good political strategy? Maybe. Since he was ruler over the northern part of a now divided kingdom, his plan for creating two new worship sites was an attempt at keeping the people loyal to him, rather than allowing them to be regularly reminded of their shared heritage with their brothers to the south each time they traveled to Jerusalem. He came up with this more convenient, more personally advantageous option, stationing an idol of gold in both Dan and Bethel, two locations that wouldn't require so much effort and travel time.

But God already had a blueprint. He had divinely ordained and sanctioned Jerusalem as the location for His people to worship Him. He'd clearly outlined that all the tribes of Israel were to return to one place to participate in their annual feasts and worship Him. (See Deut. 12:5-14.) Jeroboam chose his plans over Yahweh's to placate his own anxieties. And for this, as the next few chapters in 1 Kings attest to, he would pay a hefty price.

Is there any way in which you are currently choosing convenience or comfort over the directives of God in your life?

"He made two golden calves, and he said to the people, 'Going to Jerusalem is too difficult for you. Israel, here are your gods who brought you up from the land of Egypt.'"
1 KINGS 12:28, CSB

Committing ourselves to God's predetermined, sovereignly orchestrated plans and allowing them to govern our lives gives us a framework through which to understand His leading. Without confident trust in this biblical truth, we will lack the means to clearly hear God's voice speaking to us. Instead we will mistake our flesh's desire for ease, convenience, or pleasure as the voice of God. If left to ourselves, we will always choose "Dan" and "Bethel" over the more cumbersome journey to Jerusalem. Our flesh, if not the enemy himself, will be quick to suggest that God's way is "too difficult for you." And yet, if Jerusalem is where God's presence is, no amount of religious activity will be worth the loss of His blessing.

Being *yielded* is always a vulnerable spiritual posture, requiring a willingness to abandon your own ambitions if necessary. But it's an important commitment to make. So in regard to a situation you're currently facing, prayerfully consider where you stand: Convenience and comfort? Or commitment and obedience?

Do you really believe God already has a plan for you in this situation?

○ YES   ○ NO   ○ I'M NOT SURE

Are you willing to submit your agenda to His?

◉ YES   ○ NO   ○ I'M NOT SURE

THE PURPOSES OF GOD

As we close today's lesson, let's look closely at one of the more familiar verses you studied at the beginning of today's time. Ephesians 2:10 helps us remain encouraged in God's plans for us and how we will be able to accomplish them for His glory.

This verse makes four powerful points. You are (1) a masterpiece, (2) created anew, (3) to do good things, and (4) to act according to His plan. The version used in the margin calls you God's "workmanship,"

"We are His workmanship, created in Christ Jesus for good works, which God prepared beforehand so that we would walk in them."
EPHESIANS 2:10

but the New Living Translation paraphrases the word as "masterpiece," which paints a highly descriptive picture of what Paul was saying.

- We are priceless works, meticulously crafted by the hands of our Creator.

- He recreated us at salvation, fully equipping us in Christ and by His own Spirit to handle what God's will requires.

- We are being prepared and called to do "good works"—God-sized acts that facilitate His kingdom agenda and purposes on the earth.

- These types of activities can't be accomplished in our own power. We walk in them as Christ expresses Himself in and through us.

Which of the above is hardest for you to believe and live in accordance with? *Circle your answer.*

As you seek to hear God's voice and discover His plan, rest in His sovereignty. Relax in His omniscient, preordained plan and journey for your life. He's a good architect. He has sketched a design with detailed attention to the nuts and bolts of your existence. Your individual interests and passions can be expressed within His purposes for you, as part of His purposes for you. Sticking to the framework of what He has created will ensure an outcome that will be beyond anything you can fathom.

When He speaks, don't circumvent it or take the easy way out. If the cross you are being asked to carry feels a bit heavier than you expected, trust that He Himself intends to pick up the slack.

 Your job is to just keep walking it out.

Craft a prayer in writing as you begin this week. As the framework for your prayer, use the principle you circled above. Ask the Lord to reorient and fortify you in this regard throughout your week of study. *(Use another piece of paper or a journal, if necessary.)*

THE INVITATION

"God will not be used. His mercy and grace are infinite and His patient understanding is beyond measure, but He will not aid men in their selfish striving after personal gain. He will not help men to attain ends which, when attained, usurp the place He by every right should hold in their interest and affection."[9]

—A. W. TOZER

My grandmother was one of the most beautiful and tender souls I have ever known. I'm sure it sounds cliché to uphold your grandmother as a model of womanhood in a sea of other options. But, for me, it isn't rhetoric. It's truth. She passed away several years ago after ninety years of good, but hard, living.

The first part of her life was spent in Guyana, South America, where my mother and her siblings were born. Then slowly, my family migrated north to the U.S. where we now have extremely deep roots. During her early married years, Grandma had a tough life. Grandpa traveled a lot, leaving her at home with eight children to raise all alone. She suffered the loss of two children who were stillborn and a personal sickness in her late twenties that left her with some lifelong physical limitations.

All the while, she was fervent in prayer and faithful in her priorities as a wife and mother. And yet she had a not-so-secret desire. She wanted to be a missionary. More than anything, she wanted to travel and share Christ across the globe—maybe to a little-known, tribal village. Her heart raced with enthusiasm at the thought.

But her dream never materialized. She was, after all, a mom of eight.

Yet instead of complaining and sulking in discontentment, she looked at the busy brood milling around her skirt every day and saw that *they* were her mission field—my mom and my beloved aunts and uncles.

They all sat at her feet learning God's Word, watching her pray, and learning to pray themselves. The trajectory of their lives (and ultimately mine) was completely changed because one woman accepted what God had placed in front of her as an *invitation* to partner with Him in the purposes He'd planned for her life. I'm so grateful she didn't resist His invitation but fully invested herself in the task at hand.

In discerning God's leading, one of the most impactful requests you can make is to ask God to open up your eyes to see—to *really see*—where He is working around you and then to jump on board with it. Instead of trying to frantically (and unsuccessfully) create your own opportunities, be looking for the places where God is already moving.

The Holy Spirit reveals God's plan to you as He orchestrates the circumstances of your life. When your spiritual eyes are open to see His divine activity on the earth and your heart is stirred to engage, this is an invitation. He has allowed you to see this "open door" as a way to personally invite you to participate with Him. You don't need to know all the details of how everything will work out *before* you say yes. You just say, *yes*, up front, knowing that if He's invited you to do it, He will empower you to carry it out.

Say *yes* to His invitation.

> The Holy Spirit reveals _____ _____ to me as He orchestrates the _____ of my life.

RANDOM, NOT SO RANDOM

In 1 Samuel 9, a man named Kish lost a few donkeys and asked his not-yet-king son, Saul, to go search for them and bring them back home. Nothing particularly interesting about a task like that. It's strikingly similar to "clean your room," "wash the dishes," or "take out the trash"—one of those mindless, mundane tasks that is simply a part of living. And yet, this seemingly inconsequential task would lead to a linchpin that reoriented Saul's whole life.

> I want you to read quite a few verses in this passage from 1 Samuel 9, but it's worth your slow, meticulous attention, okay? Read verses 1-17 and then answer the following questions:

1. How many different cities and regions did Saul and his companion go through? (vv. 4-5)

2. What does Saul's statement in verse 5 reveal in regard to his feelings about the search?

3. What was their purpose for seeking Samuel, the "man of God"? (v. 6)

4. What was Samuel's purpose in meeting Saul? (v. 17)

Saul went looking for some donkeys and ended up being anointed as royalty. His mundane, frustrating, time-consuming task was actually a divinely orchestrated conduit to bigger purposes. He could not have known how God was working on the other side of this circumstance or how God was preparing and aligning events and people for his arrival. And neither can you. All you can do is fully engage in the task before you today, believing that *"all things work together for the good of those who love God, who are called according to his purpose"* (ROM. 8:28, CSB).

Never think your circumstances are disconnected from His leading and His will. He uses seemingly meaningless activities as tools to guide you toward His plans. Don't spend your time wishing you could get out of the season of life you're in. Just keep following, expecting God to walk you into His purposes or to walk you into different circumstances. When you ask Him for direction, take into account the probability that your current activities and responsibilities are already part of the path that leads you toward His purposes.

Many other people whose stories appear in Scripture stumbled along an unlikely path, smack-dab into the sovereignly arranged purposes of God. Choose at least one of the following examples that is not as familiar to you, and explore it. What came about as a result of the circumstances in each person's life?

Joseph (Gen. 37:23-28)

Moses (Ex. 3:1-4)

Ruth (Ruth 1:3-7)

Esther (Esth. 4:10-14)

Daniel (Dan. 6:6-10)

Ananias (Acts 9:10-16)

In regard to our topic today, I can think of another personality in Scripture who intrigues me. You'll remember I talked extensively about her in our opening video session. She is nameless and faceless, the details of her life shrouded in mystery. Her appearance on the landscape of the biblical narrative is brief, found in 2 Kings 5:2-3. Read it in the margin.

Do you see her? A young girl, ripped away from her life in Israel and relegated to unfamiliar surroundings, forced into the harsh treatment of slavery in Syria. This wasn't the life she would've preferred or expected, and yet for reasons she could not have clearly understood from her vantage point, there she was.

 Go back to the <u>2 Kings</u> passage and circle two things: (1) what she did, (2) what she said.

Don't miss the valuable lessons to be gleaned from this young woman's life. Despite her less than desirable circumstances, she did her job. Whether or not she was trying to escape, we don't know. But the writer is clear to note that she was serving. She invested herself in the task before her. But that wasn't all. While engaged in her duties, her eyes were opened to see her master's need for healing, and she took the opportunity to tell his wife about <u>Elisha</u> and the healing he could offer in the name of <u>Yahweh</u>.

There's no way she could have known the significant role she would play, not only in the life of this family, but in the overarching story of God's redemption plan. Centuries later, when Jesus walked the earth and began to explain the breadth of his ministry beyond the Jews to the Gentiles, He upheld Naaman's healing as an example: *"There were many lepers in Israel in the time of Elisha the prophet; and none of them was cleansed, but only Naaman the Syrian"* **(LUKE 4:27)**. Guess what: God used the spiritual sensitivity of a young girl in an unwanted place to help bring it about.

Look back at the life situations you wrote on the inside front or back cover of this book. Have you asked God to open your eyes to see His purposes within these circumstances? Is there any way in which you can already see the hand of the Lord moving or His divine purposes being served through these events?

"The Arameans had gone out in bands and had taken captive a little girl from the land of Israel; and she waited on Naaman's wife. She said to her mistress, 'I wish that my master were with the prophet who is in Samaria! Then he would cure him of his leprosy.'"
2 KINGS 5:2-3

What does this confirm about how you should proceed?

We often find God's will when we do what's next and obediently respond to the normal duties of life. The late author and Bible teacher Elisabeth Elliot said that one of the best pieces of advice she ever received in life was to "do the next thing."[10] We encounter God's guidance as we engage and invest ourselves in our current circumstances.

God is the God of right now. He calls us not to be regretful over yesterday or worried about tomorrow. He wants us focusing on what He is saying to us and putting in front of us today. The enemy's voice will focus on the past and the future; the voice of our God will focus on today and will point us confidently toward the future.

Want to know God's will for you?

Well, what has He put before you today?

Do it.

TIMING IS EVERYTHING

"This thief's voice, unlike God's voice, threatens and intimidates on the basis of fear: *If you don't do this, you'll be sorry.* It may order you or try to force you to do things. It is often urgent and pressing, sermonizing and demeaning: *Do this now! If you wait, all will be lost!*"[11]

—JAN JOHNSON

I'm impatient.

There.

I admit it.

If there is one area in which I am constantly asking God for the strength of His Spirit—although trust me, there are many, many more—here's the clear-cut winner. *Patience.* I'm a get-it-done kind of girl, ready to move forward to the next thing as soon as I know there's a "next thing" to move on to. If there's a project that needs doing, then let's get 'er done. If there's a step to take, let's take it. If there's a decision to make, why in the world haven't we made it yet?

Admittedly, my husband, Jerry, has got me beat in this department. This particular fruit of the Spirit shines through his life with glaring brilliance. That man can sit on a decision for day after painstaking day, weighing all the consequences before finally—*finally*—landing on a decision. (Lord, help me.) Yet so often God has blessed our family with protection or opportunity because Jerry led us to wait. To wait until the time was right.

> How about you? Are you naturally inclined toward patience? Or impatience? Give a short example.

> "The vision is yet for the appointed time; it hastens toward the goal and it will not fail. Though it tarries, wait for it; for it will certainly come, it will not delay."
>
> HABAKKUK 2:3

I'm coming to grips with the fact that my resistance to waiting and my natural aversion to unforeseen delays and detours can be one of my greatest hindrances to hearing God's voice and accurately discerning His plan. Impatience is a thief that robs us of the best path because we are not willing to wait for it to be revealed. Instead, we lurch forward onto whatever pathway we can find and hope for the best. Yet the purposes of God not only include specific *plans*, but also specific *timing*. He orchestrates both of them—the plans *and* the timing—the events in your life *and* the chronological framework in which they occur. Our steps are ordered. *"The mind of man plans his way, but the* LORD *directs his steps"* (**PROV. 16:9**). When He speaks, it is in concert with His perfect timing to accomplish His prescribed agenda.

When God speaks, it is in concert with His _____ _____ to accomplish His _____ _____.

TICK TOCK

Nothing catches God off guard. That's why whenever you feel rushed and hurried to make a decision, whenever your next step is not rooted in a deep confidence of inner peace, this alone is an indication that God probably has not spoken. He is never late, never behind schedule. On the contrary, He patiently and persistently gives us guidance before requiring obedience. If you feel an overwhelming urge to act spontaneously in some area of your life, pull in the reins and wait for clarity.

Read John 10:2-4 in the margin. Underline the portions that clearly characterize the way our Shepherd leads.

One of the things I underlined in this passage was that He *"leads them out."* Our Shepherd leads; He doesn't drive. One difference between the enemy's voice and the Shepherd's voice is that Jesus doesn't coerce us with fear or intimidation. He doesn't push and force. He gently guides, encourages, and woos.

○ YES ○ NO   Do you feel rushed to make a decision right now?

If so, in what way?

"He who enters by the door is a shepherd of the sheep. To him the doorkeeper opens, and the sheep hear his voice, and he calls his own sheep by name and leads them out. When he puts forth all his own, he goes ahead of them, and the sheep follow him because they know his voice."

JOHN 10:2-4

What do God's preplanned purposes suggest to you about the pressures of making rushed decisions?

If you truly believe that God will speak to you in the appropriate time, you should never feel hurried or pressured to make a decision. If you aren't clear on something, stay put. Don't move. Only when God has spoken to you will you be cued to respond in obedience. Till then? Remain committed to the last thing He told you to do to the best of your abilities. Because listen: *Waiting is not the same as inactivity. Waiting is a commitment to continue in obedience until God speaks.*

> Waiting is not the same as inactivity. Waiting is a commitment to continue in obedience until God speaks.

On those occasions when a decision must be made by a certain date or time, filter your choices through the Five Ms (p. 55), and then consider two things: Which option will (1) give God the most glory or (2) cause your relationship with Him to flourish in some specific way?

How would you answer these two questions for any specific situation of yours that's demanding a time-sensitive decision?

Many Christians—and I'm talking about the active, diligent ones—while well-intentioned in their pursuit to hear God, are living tense lives. They nervously look high and low for spiritual specifics and then grow dismayed when they can't find the answers in their own timing. Even with a clear conscience to guide them, they're sure they are somehow secretly, subtly failing God or else He'd be more forthcoming, telling them everything they want to know right now.

I want you, dear one, to trust Him—to trust His plan and His timing. Breathe deeply with the knowledge that His purposes have been specifically calculated with you and His larger designs in mind. Then allow yourself the freedom to sit back and wait, listening for His next message to come whenever He knows the time is right. Don't succumb to the anxiety of pressure. You haven't necessarily done anything wrong, and you shouldn't necessarily be doing anything else. If He hasn't said more to you yet, it's because you don't need to *know* more yet. *Trust Him in this.* Commit to doing what's right in front of you now with faithful simplicity, confident that this is the pace of God's will for your life today.

DETOURS AND DELAYS

Trusting in God's timing also gives us renewed perspective on delays. When our impatience brims to the surface, spilling over into our reality, turning us into anxiety-riddled, worry-filled, frustrated people, God's sovereignty is what quells our concerns. Delays are only detours. Life interruptions are only divine interventions that put you in position to experience not only His best for you personally, but also His larger, comprehensive plan for humanity.

> Consider Elizabeth and Zechariah's situation in Luke 1:6-7. Describe their circumstance and how it connects to today's lesson.

I wonder how long they'd waited, this couple—how many times their hopes had been dashed when Elizabeth's body confirmed month after month that she still wasn't pregnant. Their dreams had been delayed and put on hold. Again.

And yet, one day in the midst of his priestly duties, Zechariah saw an angel beside the altar of incense who said to him, *"Your petition has been heard, and your wife Elizabeth will bear you a son,"* one who *"will turn many of the sons of Israel back to the Lord their God"* **(VV. 13,16)**.

But the angel's announcement didn't stop there.

What other distinguishing characteristic did the angel reveal to Zechariah in regard to this child at the end of verse 17? What was significant about the timing of John the Baptist's birth?

From Zechariah and Elizabeth's perspective, their inability to conceive a child had perhaps seemed to make no sense. Why would God do this? How could He allow this? Yet His plan had not merely been for them to have a child but to have this child with a special mission carried out in conjunction with redemptive history. This intersection of the baby's life with divine purposes would be instrumental in the coming Messiah. Elizabeth wasn't too old. God wasn't too late. The timing was right. In fact, it was perfect. Every single delay, even every single disappointment, had been for a reason.

Consider Joseph (from the Old Testament). There are quite a few verses I want you to look up, but taking the time will be worth it. For each portion of Scripture, list the detours that could have derailed his life.

Genesis 37:23-24

Genesis 37:28

Genesis 39:1

Genesis 39:11-20

Genesis 40:14,23

How did all of these delays and disappointments ultimately position Joseph for his destiny?

Genesis 41:39-40

Genesis 42:1,6,8

Genesis 45:4-8

Genesis 50:20

"There is an appointed time for everything. And there is a time for every event under heaven" **(ECCL. 3:1)**. Not just "everything," but *your* everything. The delays that frustrate you the most, even those that come as the result of another person's carelessness or error, do not override the intentionality of God's purposes. Life's delays are often divine detours, positioning you in the best place for God's plans to be served in your life.

Are you currently facing any kind of delay or major interruption? What frustrates you the most about it right now?

How would a renewed trust in God's timing affect how you feel about it?

FREELY GIVEN

Much of our frustration in hearing God centers around the issue of *timing*. We want to know more than He wants to reveal. And we want to know it *now*. But the truth is—for me, just personally here—twenty years ago, if He had spoken to me with full details concerning the family dynamics, ministry responsibilities, and life happenings that He planned to entrust to me, I would have either run impatiently to fulfill them in the wrong timing or run as fast as possible away from them. I was neither spiritually nor emotionally equipped to handle the burden of knowing everything then. Most of the time we aren't. That's why He speaks to us progressively, on a need-to-know basis, giving us just enough light for the next step. We trust Him until He moves us on.

Listen to me: When the time is right for you to know more, He'll tell you. Until then, the things that He's already shown to be His will for you are the only things you need for victory. These are the things you need to know *now* and for which you will be held accountable *now*.

So instead of asking God to reveal His will for the next twenty years of your life, refocus your request. Ask Him to give you the courage to fully engage in what He has put before you *today*, as well as the faithfulness to stay on the path until He gives you different or new directions. Keep a firm confidence in His purposes, His plans—and His perfect timing.

> "I have many more things to say to you, but you cannot bear them now."
> JOHN 16:12

THE CHALLENGE

"The world steers you to your strengths; God works through your weaknesses. . . . Human reasoning instructs you to know your limitations and live within them. God says he will do the impossible through you."[12]

—HENRY AND RICHARD BLACKABY

I want you to start off today's lesson by thinking back over the ground we've already covered this week. We've tossed around some major themes and principles together. I've felt encouraged by it all, and I can tell you my own perspective has been reoriented as I've been studying.

Look back at your notes, and record the major themes of each day's lesson here:

Day One:

Day Two:

Day Three:

Which one has been the most impactful to you? In what specific way?

Today, let's add another layer of insight to our arsenal. I've noticed, when God speaks, His direction will rarely appease my predilection to cave to my own weaknesses, insecurities, and limitations. He doesn't confine His instructions to my natural level of comfort or capacity. Usually, in fact, if a message I am hearing challenges me and requires a more specific dependence on Him in order to be accomplished, I can detect that it is His leading. When God speaks, He frequently commissions me to do what I cannot do in my own strength alone.

Instead He *"call[s] me out upon the waters—the great unknown where feet may fail."*[13] If I am to follow Him in obedience, His Word will often compel me to step outside the comfort zone of my natural abilities and into the realm of His supernatural possibilities.

His Word compels me to step outside the comfort zone of my natural _____ and into the realm of His supernatural _____.

THE CHALLENGE OF HIS PLAN

While God will often work through your strengths and gifts, using them to accomplish His purposes, He will frequently ask you to do something you'd never do on your own. He reminded Isaiah, *"As the heavens are higher than the earth, so are My ways higher than your ways and My thoughts than your thoughts"* **(ISA. 55:9)**. When He speaks, His words will challenge you to do something outside of your normal realm of acting and thinking.

Jan Johnson writes, "If what you sense from God never contains anything that surprises you, you're probably making it up yourself. It is likely that God is speaking when what you hear sounds nothing like you, or when it is so simple or so profound you would never have thought of it."[14]

When a thought comes to you out of left field, don't ignore it. Check inward to see if the Holy Spirit is encouraging you to pursue it. I often know God is speaking when a thought occurs to me that makes me feel surprised, maybe even uncomfortable, because I know I can't do it in my own power. Then, when the Holy Spirit brings conviction that will not let me rest until I move forward, I know it is God.

- Noah was asked to build an ark for surviving a flood one hundred and twenty years away.

- Abraham was asked to leave his home for an unknown country.

- Samuel was asked to give a tough message to his mentor, Eli.

- Esther was asked to plead the case for her people before a king.

- Mary was asked to become the mother of the Messiah.

Dig deeper into the following examples. Read the accompanying passage, and record how God's instructions challenged the listener.

Moses (Ex. 3:1-10)

> "If You are the Son of God, command that these stones become bread."
> MATTHEW 4:3

Gideon (Judg. 6:12-14)

> "If You are the Son of God, throw Yourself down; for it is written, 'He will command His angels concerning you'; and 'On their hands they will bear You up, so that You will not strike Your foot against a stone.'"
> MATTHEW 4:6

Rich man (Luke 18:18-23)

Circle the passage that has a similar theme or tone to something you're currently facing.

In Matthew 4, Satan tried to get the Messiah to cop out on what the Father wanted to accomplish.

> "All these things I will give You, if You fall down and worship me."
> MATTHEW 4:9

Look at the selected verses in the margin from Matthew 4, taken from the time when Jesus was led into the wilderness by God's Spirit (don't miss that important point from verse 1) to endure challenge. For each sentiment listed below, describe how the enemy's suggestion tempted Jesus to satisfy it.

- Appease fleshly appetites _____

- Receive attention and admiration _____

- Avoid death and suffering _____

The voices of our enemy, our pride, our apathy, or even our own egos will always give us the easier option. Their suggestions will always seek to circumvent God's way with the promise of ease, shortcuts, and immediate gratification. They will never encourage us to stay the course, see our commitment through to the end, or tap into divine resources along the way. They will encourage us to hide our weakness and frailty instead of offering them to Jesus.

But shortcuts are not usually God's way. He puts extraordinary tasks on the plates of ordinary people so that ordinary people can see what an extraordinary God can do through them.

> How might your decision to choose the more challenging road make room for God's power to be seen in you? Or for your dependence on Him to increase? *Plan to discuss this with your small group.*

> Pause for a moment and talk to the Lord about what you've written above. Ask Him to give you His peace and courage to accept any challenge that represents His best for you.

If given an option easier than what God asks of us, we are understandably inclined to take it. Who wants more trouble than they've already got? But God's voice commands the option that will display His power. And "easy" doesn't always provide the right backdrop for that kind of miraculous display. He desires to show Himself strong in you and will encourage you to do things that require trust and faith. The enemy's voice says, "You don't have enough. You're not able. You can't." The voice of the Holy Spirit says, "I have enough. I am able through you. I can!"

When you face two options and each seems to please God, consider the one that will display God's glory, power, and strength instead of yours. This makes room for God to reveal Himself to you and show Himself through you.

A FINAL WORD

Please hear me clearly. I'm not suggesting that God's way is *never* easy, *never* comfortable, and *always* as hard as it could possibly be. What I am saying is that when conviction stirs in your heart toward something difficult or doggone near impossible, remember—this is often a sign of His direction. Your own flesh or ego would never compel you to do something that it knows it cannot do. Your own mind would always seek to convince you to stay in the safety zone where the path is proven and your capabilities are well-tested. And yet if the conviction persists and the peace of God rules in your heart, turn your attention upward.

I've got to be honest with you—this characteristic of God's voice has become one of the most significant ways that I recognize His leading in my own life. It's been a pattern in His dealings with me. When I look back at where He has taken me in ministry, every stage of it has been built on one challenge after another. At every single point when our ministry moved to a new dimension, we were asked to cross a sturdy bridge of faith to get there.

Most often I was highly intimidated by what the Lord was telling me to do. I felt incapable, afraid, overwhelmed, and ill-equipped for the task. (Including the task of writing, for example. Like writing Bible studies. Like the one you're holding in your hand right now.)

Yet I'm continually working to quell the voice that wants to take the easy road out. (*Quit. Don't even try. You're not good enough. You can't.*) And I'm constantly asking God to give me peace to walk down any road He intends for me, despite whatever challenge might lay ahead.

But here's the thing: whenever I've just gone along with Him, He has never failed to show up right on time, giving me exactly what I need. I may not always agree with His plans initially, but I am learning to trust Him anyway. Keeping a record of our history together continues to buoy my faith in the future.

God wants you to see the wondrous things He will accomplish in you. Don't be fearful about the hard road He may ask you to take. Be encouraged and excited about seeing His divine, supernatural activity in and through you.

One of the best faith-building things I've ever done is to keep a running list of challenging tasks that I've clearly seen the Lord accomplish through me. End today's lesson by using the journaling lines below to chronicle a handful of difficult things you've stepped out in faith to accomplish. How did the Lord show His strength in your weakness? How does this fortify your resolve for future obedience?

_____

_____

_____

_____

_____

_____

_____

_____

_____

_____

_____

_____

_____

_____

_____

_____

_____

_____

_____

_____

_____

_____

THE FIFTH DAY

Unlocking God's purposes for your life rests largely in what we've studied this week. Making the connection between God's voice and His plan is a major key in discerning His leading. Many times, hearing Him is less about what you *hear* and more about what you *see*—His fingerprints, His handiwork, His plans unfolding before you. This is your invitation.

His voice will always reflect His plans—plans that are always bigger than ours, always better, always on time, and, yes, frequently more demanding than we'd prefer. Yet the blessing He offers when we trust Him is far greater than we'd expect as well. Even when others don't see what you find so fruitful and positive about following Him—even if you don't see it yourself on some days—the gift of simply being able to stay close to Him, close to His heart, and close to His eternal purposes at work in your life is more than a lot of people ever get to experience. Oh, what they miss by thinking their plans are so much more important, fulfilling, and long-lasting.

If He's captured your heart this week with a renewed passion for pursuing His plans and purposes, let the example of Jesus instruct you as you proceed in humble obedience.

> Look up John 5:19 in your Bible, and paraphrase it here in your own words. How would this action that Jesus described look when applied to your own life?

Jesus not only did His Father's will, but get this: He did the Father's will *and nothing else*! He didn't create new ideas or strike out on His own. He simply recognized the Father's will and then followed up on it. And we can do the same thing. No need for further complicating things. No need for worrying we're maybe missing out on something.

No need for figuring how to get God's will and our will accomplished in the same calendar day. Whatever He says, we do it. Wherever He shows us He's working and inviting us to join Him, we go there. To serve Him.

> Read John 12:26 in the margin. Underline two things this verse reveals about God's true servants.

I am strongly convicted by the principles of this passage. True servants of God follow Him and go where He goes. End of discussion. And the beginning of a more purposeful life.

God wants to reveal Himself and His plans to you. *Wants* to. He is *inviting* you there. So stay attentive, keeping your spiritual eyes peeled for His purposes. When He allows you to see His activity in the circumstances of your life, you have heard the voice of God. Use your time on this Fifth Day to ask the Lord in prayer, and even on paper, to open up your spiritual eyes so that you'll never again miss His divine invitation.

"If anyone serves Me, he must follow Me; and where I am, there My servant will be also; if anyone serves Me, the Father will honor him."
JOHN 12:26

THE CHURCH CONNECTION
by Dr. Tony Evans

God's voice has an overriding purpose: to bring Him glory through the advancement of His kingdom. All of Scripture is tied to this goal. If this is not our goal as well, we are ill-aligned with His ultimate plans for our lives, which naturally results in our not being able to hear His voice clearly.

The church is God's primary agent for achieving His chief goal. Its overriding responsibility is to represent and advance God's kingdom program in history (Matt. 16:18-19). That's why it saddens me as a pastor when I meet Christians who are detached from the church because I know they are are operating outside of God's plan, and as such will not be well positioned to hear His voice. Since He speaks the loudest within this divinely established community, disconnected Christians are less likely to know His agenda and their part in it. The concept of church as being little more than a weekly place where we go to receive spiritual information and inspiration falls far beneath its purpose. The church exists to cooperate with God's kingdom agenda. This is why believers are told not to forsake assembling themselves together with other believers (Heb. 10:23-25). To intentionally do so is to operate in rebellion.

The Bible refers to the church as a *"body"* **(1 COR. 12:13)**. Christ, as head of the body (Eph. 1:22-23), communicates to the various parts what their functions are to be in fulfilling His kingdom purpose for their lives. But no individual part can receive instruction from the head if it is detached from the rest of the body. Communication from God takes place in the context of spiritual attachment with others. In Acts 13:1-4, the Holy Spirit spoke during a worship experience and gave clear direction for the work He wanted Paul and Barnabas to do for His kingdom purpose. This story in Acts demonstrates that His voice through the church is not limited to what happens in the pulpit but extends also to what happens in the pew, as the body grows through that which *"every joint supplies"* **(EPH. 4:16)**. We all are involved together in hearing from Him, just as when our brain instructs a part of our body to function. Other connected body parts (nerves) convey the message, while still others (muscles) assist in getting the job done. Every part matters.

As a thriving member of the church, you are not simply a cul-de-sac Christian but rather a conduit believer that He can use to be a blessing to others. Being connected to the church (as opposed to merely attending church) frees the Holy Spirit to speak. Throughout the forty-plus years of our congregation in Dallas, we have often heard members tell of how God gave them direction, clarified a decision, reversed a course, or confirmed a plan in their lives. I truly believe when God sees He can work through you to *be* a blessing, not just *receive* a blessing, He is much more apt to speak to you, trusting you with His insight and instruction. God can expand and increase your life in many ways by being a functioning member of your local church—not the least of which is your ability to hear, discern, and confirm His will for your life.

163

A Continual State of Readiness

WEEK SIX

The one thing is relationship with Jesus Christ.

"My _____ hear My voice, and I _____ them, and they

_____ _____ ..." **JOHN 10:27**

1. The Relationship—My sheep

   When you become a believer, you become a part of the _____

   _____ _____.

   "Therefore you are no longer outsiders (exiles, migrants, and
   aliens, excluded from the rights of citizens), but you now share
   citizenship with the saints (God's own people, consecrated and
   set apart for Himself); and you belong to God's [own] household."
   EPHESIANS 2:19 (AMPCE)

2. The Result—Hear My voice

   _____ *God to speak.*

   _____ *and* _____ *are divine interruptions.*

3. The Reason—I know them

   "When I talk, nothing happens; when God talks, the universe comes
   into existence."[1] **BOB SORGE**

4. The Response—They follow Me

   He is your _____ *Shepherd. (Heb. 13:20)*

GREAT EXPECTATIONS

"God will speak to the hearts of those who prepare themselves to hear; and conversely, those who do not so prepare themselves will hear nothing even though the Word of God is falling upon their outer ears every Sunday."[2]

—A. W. TOZER

I hope you're still feeling hungry—spiritually speaking—wishing this weren't our last week of study, wanting more of the closeness and connection you've been experiencing with God during these hours that we've been poised on the edge of our seats to hear Him.

That's exactly how you're supposed to feel.

Because once you hear His voice, regular mundane versions of Christianity will never satisfy you again. You'll want to remain in a spiritual posture that invites a continual invasion of His manifest presence. You'll want to keep rolling out the red carpet of holy invitation. You'll want to be proactively, consistently confirming your alignment with Him, continually seeking Him in His Word—listening, looking, heeding, and hearkening—your spiritual senses piqued to recognize and discern when He is speaking. Any distance or dryness that threatens the gushing well of God's Spirit in your life will feel like the worst of illnesses from now on. All you'll want to do is get over it and get on with it—back to the business of close, intimate, active relationship with God.

This, in fact, is where clear communication with God begins—a believer approaching her relationship with Him from an ongoing stance of anticipation, readied and expectant to hear His voice.

Consider three important words drawn from this last sentence.

- Anticipation
- Readiness
- Expectation

In one or two sentences, describe how you think this type of stance looks in the life of a believer.

Now personalize your response. In what ways do you show anticipation, readiness, and expectation in hearing God speak?

In what ways, if any, are you a bit apathetic, indifferent, or dispassionate?

It's our last week here. The first week of the rest of our lives. Let's spend it growing in anticipation, readiness, and hope-filled expectation. And let's start it by meeting up with an old friend named:

HABAKKUK

We know very little about Habakkuk, except for his easily misspelled name and the few inferences he makes toward himself in his Old Testament book. He was a prophet to God's people who had deep convictions regarding his faith and prevailing sensitivities about the injustices within his society. Scholars suggest he may have had some kind of responsibility as a temple musician, given the musical descriptions that appear in his third chapter. Apparently he was a man of diverse interests and talents. And yet when his book opens, he is utterly consumed by one driving focus—to hear from God.

Read Habakkuk 1:2-3; see the margin. Describe the tone of Habakkuk's plea. Record the keywords from the passage that lead you to this conclusion.

"How long, LORD, must I call for help and you do not listen or cry out to you about violence and you do not save? Why do you force me to look at injustice? Why do you tolerate wrongdoing?"
HABAKKUK 1:2-3, CSB

What does this tell you about the prophet's emotional state at the time?

In your most recent conversations with God, what has your overarching tone been like? *(Circle any that apply.)*

- Grateful
- Discouraged
- Hopeful
- Remorseful
- Repentant
- Joyous
- Meditative
- Other _____

Habakkuk's key questions—*"How long?"* **(V. 2)** and *"Why?"* **(V. 3)**—are a clear indicator of the sentiments in his heart. Aren't these the same two questions that haunt us as well, when the circumstances of life seem to be closing in on us with no detectable end in sight? Particularly when we've been praying about the same things for an extended period of time, waiting on God to give any indication that He has heard us or even cares, we can become discouraged and depleted of hope. *Why? How long?* The divine silence scares us. It makes us feel despondent. Ignored. Apathy threatens to set in, making us callous, bitter, and hardened. More than anything during these times, we want to know *how long* we must continue calling out to Him, and *why* He would allow these circumstances we're facing to go on.

Think of a request you've been bringing to the Lord for a long time. It's quite possibly the same issue you've kept at the forefront of your thoughts throughout this entire study. Use the prompts on the next page to help you fill in some of your questions to the Lord regarding this circumstance.

How long . . .

Why . . .

In light of your real questions and concerns, do you still expect God to respond and speak to you? Or are you losing hope instead? Write your honest thoughts below.

If you are feeling a bit tired and despondent, how has this loss of hope affected:

- Your relationship with God

- Your interest in prayer

- Your outlook on other areas of difficulty in your life

- Your connectedness within the church

- Your spiritual sensitivity toward God's activity around you

- Your sense of gratitude

What else would you add to this list?

We don't know how long Habakkuk had been calling out to God. But when God didn't seem to be answering, we do know this: Habakkuk pointed an accusatory finger. He started to lose confidence that the Lord would ever answer him.

Today, I want you to see the fact that Habakkuk questioned God, as we ourselves sometimes question God—but not only that. What I want you to see is that when God *did* give His answer (beginning in verse 5), He didn't angrily scold this man who dared question the Lord's interest and involvement in these situations. Please do not let the beauty of God's grace go unnoticed here. Yahweh heard Habakkuk's questions, but He received them mercifully and patiently.

So those questions you wrote down? When I prompted you to capture your "why" and "how long" complaints? Don't go back and scratch through them, afraid you've offended God by asking them, even more by writing them down! No, He's received *your* questions with grace too—even the questions that remain tucked inside your heart, unshared, unspoken, unwritten. In His vast kindness toward us, in His knowledge of our frailty, God lets us ask our questions.

And He may just answer them in even bigger and bolder ways than we've asked them.

> Read Habakkuk 1:5 in the margin, and underline the action verbs—the actions that God commanded Habakkuk to take.

What an answer, huh? God wasn't off twiddling His thumbs some-where, paying no attention. He was already answering! Habakkuk hadn't seen it because he'd been looking elsewhere.

A wider vision changes everything. Doesn't it? Because if we're looking—I mean, really looking—we'll see the traces of God's hand all around us. Already speaking, already moving, already working things into the shape of His own wise will and providence.

And what was true for Habakkuk was also true for—Esther.

"Look among the nations! Observe! Be astonished! Wonder! Because I am doing something in your days— you would not believe if you were told."
HABAKKUK 1:5

ESTHER

We'll return to Habakkuk's story tomorrow. But I want to take a sharp U-turn in your Bible to another portion of Scripture that punctuates the point I'm hoping will settle into your heart today.

I suspect you know much of Esther's story already. Please bear with me while I share a simple overview with you again, and then ask you to consider a small portion of the narrative that relates to what we're talking about.

This book of the Bible is the breathtaking saga of a young Jewish girl gifted with an unfair amount of beauty. When the King of Persia hosted a pageant to determine who his new wife would be, Esther was the one who caught his eye and ultimately his heart. Whatever she wanted, he desired to give her, *"even to half of the kingdom"* **(ESTH. 5:3)**.

When a plot to annihilate the Jews was uncovered, Esther's cousin, Mordecai, stepped in to remind her of the providential hand of Almighty God in giving her such favor with Persia's king. You'll remember Mordecai's famous, poetic line, *"Who knows whether you have not come to the kingdom for such a time as this?"* **(4:14, ESV)**.

Indeed she had—because Mordecai's life was in danger, along with all the Jewish people (Esther included). His nemesis, Haman, a high-ranking official in the palace (who'd actually cooked up this genocidal plot in the first place), hated him for his allegiance to Yahweh and his refusal to bow and scrape before Haman at public appearances—hated him enough to hastily build a gallows specifically for use in hanging this man who got under his skin so much.

Through all of this, Yahweh seemed oddly disengaged. In fact, His name is not even mentioned in the entire book. And yet to the one who has spiritual vision, His fingerprints and providential guidance are all over it, from the first chapter till the last. One particular portion of this story, I think, illustrates this reality the best.

Dig into Esther 6, starting right at the beginning, and look for answers to the following questions on the next page.

1. What couldn't the king seem to do on this specific night—the night after Haman concocted his plan to kill Mordecai? (v. 1)

2. What did he ask for to help cure his insomnia? (v. 1)

3. What did he discover during his reading? (v. 2)

4. How did he respond in light of this newfound knowledge? (v. 3)

5. Who happened to be in the king's courtyard at this exact moment? And why was he there? (v. 4)

6. What did the king ask him? (v. 6)

7. Given Haman's elevated view of himself, who did he assume the king was referring to? (v. 6)

I just love this. Look at the thread of "coincidental" happenings woven into the story. To the spiritually insensitive eye, all these details are merely fortuitous events. Products of sheer luck. There's no trace of God, His hand, or even His interest in the devastation about to befall Mordecai and the entire Jewish race. And yet:

- The king can't sleep?

- He looks for something to read?

- He comes across a record of Mordecai's past service to him?

- Haman shows up, seeking permission to put Mordecai to death?

- The king, not knowing this—in fact, seeking counsel on how to honor Mordecai—poses a question that Haman is easily able to misunderstand?

- And, in answering it mistakenly, Haman sets a ball rolling that leads to his own demise, the elevation of Mordecai, and the salvation of the Jews?

This kind of stuff "just happens"?

Yes—when God is involved in it—just as He's involved with you now, right here in the midst of your hurts, fears, and disappointments. Whether or not you perceive Him at work depends largely on whether you're postured to "look, observe, be astonished, and wonder"—to be expectantly hopeful and eager for Him, believing He's at work even when He seems distant.

Yes, ask Him your questions. *How long, Lord? Why, Lord?* But then immediately ask Him for vision to recognize where His providential hand is already at work. Your personal problem (though important, simply because it's yours) is but a small sliver in the grand scope of all God is doing.

Broaden your vantage point, and prepare to be amazed at what He's already doing.

PATIENCE PLEASE

"It takes greater faith and devotion to pray, trust, and obey when God is absent than when He is present."[3]

—R. T. KENDALL

Scripture paints a picture of intentional relationship between God and man, a friendship in which two-way communication unfolds. We cry out, He listens. We cry out, and in His own timing, He answers. We *don't* see a pattern of people calling out to God and then walking away despairing, assuming God won't respond. They believed if they were seeking His guidance, He would supply it. They looked expectantly and eagerly for the response He would offer.

The emphasis in modern times on instant gratification has left us depleted and anemic in our faith. Any passage of time that elapses between our prayers and God's response turns us into doubters, questioning and quivering in our spiritual boots. We claim to believe God speaks, but we are secretly discouraged and doubtful when we don't see immediate evidence of His work or hear His voice quickly enough to suit our personally engineered timeline.

This may be *our* view, but it is not the *biblical* view.

My prayer is that throughout these weeks together, our resolve has been strengthened. We're determined not to be weak, feeble women who are easily discouraged or led astray. We are ready to stand firm in our faith, our eyes glued to the prize of His presence, our hearts brimming with hopeful anticipation of His promises to us as His daughters. He is near. He is present. He speaks!

Just as He spoke to Habakkuk—so let's return to his example today.

With fresh perspective on God's activity around him, as a result of the invitation to "look" and "observe," Habakkuk's confidence was renewed and rebuilt. Fitted with the vision required to see how God was weaving events both large and small into an answer—a hard answer, yes, but an answer just the same—he was assured of God's ability and sovereignty despite the continued devastation around him.

Right away, you can tell the difference in Habakkuk's heart.

> Read Habakkuk 1:12-13 in the margin. Compare and contrast this with his first prayer that you studied yesterday. How is the tone of the latter prayer different than the former?

> What is clearly missing from the first prayer that is evident in the second?

When our eyes are open to detect God's fingerprints of providence, when our hearts are reminded of His never-ending care for us, our internal posture becomes reframed and our conversations with Him are transformed. Like Habakkuk, the focus, tone, and even the intention of our prayers are redirected more into alignment with God's will and His priorities. Instead of offering a string of requests born out of disappointments and frustrations, we pause in His presence and—*we see Him.*

In this way, prayer becomes more of what it was intended to be—a key to unlock the ways of heaven onto the landscape of earth—instead of a manipulative exercise in which we hope to force the Lord's hand to do what we want. Prayer becomes less about what *we want* and more about who *He is.*

Listen to author John Powell describe this beautiful exchange, how the Lord "widens my vision, helps me see what is really important in life, and to distinguish the really important from the unimportant. . . . He comes to me, in the listening, receptive moments of prayer, and he transfuses his power into me."[4]

"Are You not from everlasting, O Lord, my God, my Holy One? We will not die. You, O Lord, have appointed them to judge; and You, O Rock, have established them to correct. Your eyes are too pure to approve evil, and You cannot look on wickedness with favor. Why do You look with favor on those who deal treacherously? Why are You silent when the wicked swallow up those more righteous than they?"

HABAKKUK 1:12-13

By widening our vision, by hearing Him, He changes us.

Habakkuk's second prayer was completely different from his first. After seeing his circumstances through new eyes, his focus shifted. Instead of primarily viewing the devastation *around* him, he now focused on his God *before* him. Earlier, when he'd been consumed with *how long* and *why*, there was no mention of God's attributes in his prayer. But now, from a new perspective, with his heart tenderized by what he'd seen of God's sovereign work, his prayer highlights the power of God. He has reframed his prayer into one that now anticipates divine intervention.

Think of the line below as a continuum which maps out the shift in tone from Habakkuk's first prayer to the second. Determine where you think your heart is located on this spectrum in regard to your own spiritual posture and outlook.

|———————————————————————————|

first prayer (vv. 2-3)   second prayer (vv. 12-13)
doubtful and accusatory   *expectant and confident*

Because Habakkuk's approach to God has changed, God's approach to Habakkuk changes as well. In His first answer (1:5-11), God spoke primarily to prove He was indeed up to something, to build the prophet's confidence. But the second time—with Habakkuk's perspective shifted from doubtful and cynical to honoring and expectant—God spoke to give him actual instructions and guidance regarding the situation at hand (2:2-20).

Indeed, the way we pray and the posture of our hearts in prayer are key factors in receiving guidance from God.

• *Everlasting*

• *Holy*

• *Our Rock*

• *Pure*

In the margin, I've listed some of the key attributes of God mentioned in Habakkuk's second prayer. Use these words (and others that come to mind) to write a short prayer refocusing your attention on God, on His control of your circumstances, and on your confidence in His desire to speak to you regarding them. Write your prayer on a separate piece of paper or an index card, and post it in a strategic location where you can see it often and be reminded of God's faithfulness and good intentions toward you. Push past any internal resistance you may feel. Pray and believe. Worship. And wait.

ON THE WATCHTOWER

Habakkuk's tone in prayer wasn't the only thing that shifted in his posture toward communication with Yahweh.

Below, write Habakkuk 2:1 verbatim from your Bible.

The Hebrew word for stand is amad. It means to endure, remain and to be standing both in body and attitude.[5]

Given the definitions in the margin, what other words would you use to describe Habakkuk's stance while waiting on God's response?

The Hebrew word for station is yatsab. It means "to take one's stand."[6]

How does this compare with your usual posture toward hearing God?

In Habakkuk's day, a military watchman minimized all distractions so he could concentrate fully on the task of protecting the city from approaching forces. He would elevate himself on a tower placed strategically and intentionally so that his eyes could be peeled on the horizon without his attention being diverted to any movements on the ground, which could easily instill anxiety. The watchman's goal was to catch the first sight of a coming enemy or a returning king. From this height, his vantage point was broad, his perspective unique from those below. This was serious work, deserving of devoted attention. The guard would not allow anyone to coerce him from his post or from the eagle-eyed execution of his duties.

In the previous paragraph, underline the main purposes and benefits of the watchtower in military strategy.

Habakkuk deliberately chose these military terms to describe his posture when waiting on God. This is how much he valued communication from Yahweh and how important he knew the spiritual virtue of patience to be in receiving it. He was purposeful and resolved, vigilant and tenacious. He *knew* his God would answer, so he positioned himself proactively to receive it. Till then, he would wait. Patiently. On the watchtower.

How do some of these postures translate to your spiritual life?

- Standing on the guard post

- Stationing yourself on the watchtower *(some translations say "rampart")*

- Keeping watch

Name some specific, proactive ways that you can incorporate these postures into your life within the next 24 hours.

Who can help keep you accountable to this vigilant spiritual stance?

All of these postures are active. They require resolve. They are not for the lazy or the faint of heart.

Nor are they for the *impatient.*

We are always willing to wait on things that are important to us. We will stay by our phones awaiting a call if it's regarding a career opportunity or a report from the doctor's office. We will wait in line to buy much-needed groceries for our family. We will wait out the long months before the arrival of a baby. The value we place on an object or person dictates the amount of time and the vigilant posture we're willing to take when waiting on them.

Habakkuk wasn't budging. He just waited on God—his posture militant, his stance strong, and his resolve sure. He determined not to make a move until he received divine direction. If we value God's voice as Habakkuk did, we should be willing to wait for it—*patiently*—trusting in His sovereign timing, standing firm until we've received it.

This virtue of patience would be so critical to Habakkuk that God buffered His guidance with the words recorded in Habakkuk 2:3 (in the margin). It was a stern lesson to Habakkuk about the importance of patience in carrying out God's plan, encouraging him to relax in God's sovereignty.

> God encouraged Habakkuk to be patient by assuring him of four specific promises regarding the vision He was about to reveal. Underline them in the margin, and then rewrite them in your own words below.

1. The time was _____.

2. _____ for it.

3. It will _____ _____.

4. It will not _____.

"The vision is yet for the appointed time; it hastens toward the goal and it will not fail. Though it tarries, wait for it; for it will certainly come, it will not delay."
HABAKKUK 2:3

Claim these truths for yourself! Great relief awaits those who stand firmly on the promises in this verse. God's plan for you will come to pass in its appointed time. He Himself will assure it. Rest and trust. Cease striving and know that He is God (Ps. 46:10). Be free from the burden of trying to make things happen, and trust that your God loves you and will fulfill His word for your life.

LISTEN IN

"Things don't change when I talk to God; things change when God talks to me."[7]

—BOB SORGE

I'm getting old.

And that's okay. I'm not averse to it, just aware of it.

As the years roll on, I'm changing in more ways than I can count, in all aspects of my life—physically, emotionally, and mentally. Most of it I'm enjoying. Some of it (like aching joints) I'm finding a bit annoying.

But one of the clearest transformations I'm seeing in myself is an increased attraction to *simplicity*. Any opportunity I find to minimize complicated matters or reduce our physical inventory of collected things, I take it. Whether I'm cleaning out a closet or simply resisting the urge to fill every square inch of margin on my calendar, I can almost feel a literal weight being lifted off of me. Where I once strived for fullness, I now value emptiness. Silence, solitude, and simplicity—I cherish these things in ways I never did during my younger years.

The same thing is true when it comes to words. I'm discovering that less is best. I've never been a shy person—never been one of those people who couldn't think of something to say—and, I assure you, I'm still an extrovert. Love a good conversation. But unlike any other season in my life, I've begun to value listening. I mean *really listening*. I'm recognizing what a gift it is to the person who's talking. But even more, I'm discovering the blessing of being the listener, because silence creates the margin into which others can speak into *my* life— offering wisdom, extending comfort, sharing insights, revealing all kinds of helpful information I truly need to hear. But *wouldn't* hear—if I wasn't listening.

"Do not be hasty in word or impulsive in thought to bring up a matter in the presence of God. For God is in heaven and you are on the earth; therefore let your words be few."
ECCLESIASTES 5:2

The Old Testament prophets had unique experiences, but seeing Habakkuk climb that watchtower to find the silence and solitude he needed to await God's word is a tender moment in Scripture for me. It reminds me how difficult these two treasures—*silence, solitude*—are to find, both then and now. Impossible really, unless we occasionally do what the prophet did—climb up and away from the mind-numbing pace of life, creating the space and margin into which God can interject His thoughts and plans. The practice of simply being *still* has almost been totally lost. And we are paying the price for it—not only in fatigued, unhealthy bodies but in shriveled, starved, depleted spirits.

They're the hard results of not *listening* for the voice of God.

> Scripture repeats the pattern of God calling His people away from constant action to the proactive stance of stillness. Circle the phrase in Habakkuk 2:20 (in the margin) that reveals the *reason* for silence, then put a box around the phrases in Psalm 46:10 and Isaiah 30:15 that explain the *result* of silence.
>
> What other results do we deny ourselves when we refuse pockets of silence and stillness in our lives?

Could it be we don't hear God much today because we've trained ourselves *not* to hear Him? Not only have we succumbed (even aspired) to our busy lifestyles, but we've learned to interpret any in-between spaces of silence as triggers to feed our activity hunger even more—checking our phones, accessing the day's news, catching up on things, seeing who else might be wanting us—when, yes, *God* is wanting us. Wanting to sit with us. Wanting to talk to us.

If you're feeling the tug and strain of it all today, if you're feeling your strength and peace and alertness just draining away from you in mad rushes of busy, distracted multitasking, it's time we all heard this: None of those precious things are coming back to us until we hear from God. None of us will be hearing from God in a consistent, ongoing fashion until we consciously, deliberately clear away the

"The LORD is in His holy temple. Let all the earth be silent before Him."
HABAKKUK 2:20

"Be still, and know that I am God."
PSALM 46:10, ESV

"The Lord GOD, the Holy One of Israel, has said, 'In repentance and rest you will be saved, in quietness and trust is your strength.'"
ISAIAH 30:15

clutter, create the margin, and tune our attention inward to listen for what His Spirit is saying.

But there's a path back to where you and I each want to be. We can reverse and reclaim the things that have squelched the clear voice of God in our ears, dampened it to the point where we don't even recognize it anymore. We must carve out time to purposefully listen for His voice (1) through prayer, (2) meditating on His Word, and (3) lingering worshipfully in His presence.

> I must carve out time to purposefully listen for God's voice
> through _____, _____ on His
> Word, and _____ _____ _____
> _____ _____.

PRAYER

For most of my Christian life, I got up from my prayer time feeling like I'd sat through a one-way conversation and received absolutely no response. Prayer was a busy exercise filled with my own interests and personal desires. Yet I knew there had to be more. I desperately longed for a real encounter with God. I believed He wanted more out of my prayer life with Him and so did I. That's when I began to take seriously the art of listening, making prayer more about God and less about me.

Listening to God in prayer involves your full participation. You must engage your body, mind, and spirit. In her book *Listening to God*, Joyce Huggett describes how she closes her eyes "to shut out visual stimuli," how she closes her ears by "dealing authoritatively" with distractions, how she closes "a series of shutters on the surface level of my life, thus holding at bay hindrances to hearing the still, small voice of God."[8]

> List the "visual stimuli" that normally distract you from tuning in to God. Then go back and list some conscious efforts you can make to remove those distractions. *(Use a separate sheet of paper if you need more room.)*

What do you think "dealing authoritatively with distractions" means?

In 1 Corinthians 14:15, the apostle Paul said he prayed with his mind and also with his spirit. This first kind of prayer—praying with my mind—is what I do most often. I work through my prayer list. I ask for forgiveness of sins. I offer Him thanks for specific things. I bring Him needs for which I desire His intervention. I intercede on behalf of others. All of these are good and proper, important aspects of prayer.

But instead of getting up and leaving after I've covered all the items on my prayer list, I've learned to wait. To quiet my mind. To move into a Spirit-led time of prayer. Spirit-led prayer gives the Holy Spirit the opportunity (not just me) to direct my prayer time.

> Read 1 Corinthians 2:10-12 in your Bible. According to this passage, why do we need to connect with the Spirit during prayer? Write your answer in the margin.

The Spirit knows the thoughts of God and can express them as He leads me in prayer. When I embark on this journey in my prayer time, I turn my thoughts completely on Him, on what He is saying to me.

He'll often bring to mind people or situations about which I might not normally think—and I turn those thoughts into prayer. He'll call sins to mind that I didn't realize or had forgotten about—and I turn those thoughts into prayer. He'll bring a specific verse to my mind, or He'll direct me to worship, based on a specific characteristic or attribute of God—and I turn it all into prayer.

"I will pray with the spirit," Paul said, "and I will pray with the mind also" (1 COR. 14:15). And in so doing, we truly begin to hear God.

MEDITATION

Some of my most precious times with God come not during corporate worship experiences (as important as those are) but during times of personal meditation. When I say *meditation*, I'm not referring to mystical, navel-gazing exercises designed to empty the mind (for who knows what to come in). I'm talking instead about being silent before the true and living God, meditating on Him as His Word calls believers to do.

My Bible and journal are my only companions during these times. I normally just sit still in His presence, sometimes in silence, sometimes with a specific Bible verse on my mind. But not exactly to pray. Just to listen.

Meditation is a discipline because it requires me to control my desire to fill the silence with activity. I simply sit, think, and ponder. I may concentrate on Scripture, on the goodness of God to me, or merely on the goodness of God Himself, in general.

I typically write down the thoughts the Holy Spirit brings to my mind, wanting to capture any messages that I sense the Lord leading me to hear from Him through His Word. If my to-do list starts to infringe, tempting to sidetrack my attention, I "deal authoritatively" with the distraction, writing a note to myself in the margin of my journal or typing it into my cell phone so I won't forget it. Then I go immediately back to the more important task of listening to God, because that's what I came for—to meditate on Him and His Word alone.

> Stop now for a short time of meditation. Turn to Isaiah 50:4-5, and read it slowly and personally. Put your name into the verse as you read it, and record in your journal or on a separate sheet of paper any thoughts the Lord brings to mind as you meditate. Deal "authoritatively" with any distractions.

WORSHIP

Meditation often leads to spontaneous worship. Or it can *start* with worship. Music that honors and highlights the attributes of God can support the most wonderful and personal worship experiences. I use it frequently as a backdrop for my time with God. As the worship music speaks of His attributes, I ponder the lyrics and allow them to lead

"I shall lift up my hands to Your commandments, which I love; and I will meditate on Your statutes."
PSALM 119:48

"My eyes anticipate the night watches, that I may meditate on Your word."
PSALM 119:148

me into personal worship. The music envelops me. I am both over-whelmed and encouraged by an awareness of His presence.

As I sit, I begin to hear God—not always with specific instructions, but with a sense of His presence guiding, leading, and pursuing me wholeheartedly. He shows me how He wants to be worshiped and how I should spend my time with Him. I sense that He is with me, near me, as the words of the passage on which I am meditating come alive. In praise. Awed by His power. Comforted by His unfailing faithfulness. Humbled beyond words to be called His child.

That's how I often pray, meditate, and worship.

By sharing these details about my quiet time with you, I'm not intending to prescribe a formula for you to follow. This is not a "one-size-fits-all" program. The experience is different for each person. And it should be! Just as intimacy between a husband and wife doesn't need to be preplanned to the last detail, neither does your intimate time with the Lord. He wants to deal with you as an individual. But I do pray that some of these observations will provide an encour-aging roadmap for you in developing a conversational relationship with God, one that will become a key building block of your life, long after this Bible study has come to an end.

By listening to God through prayer, meditation, and worship, the Holy Spirit will begin to speak to you, revealing God's personal and timely word for your life.

A RETURN TO OBEDIENCE

"People do not drift toward holiness. Apart from grace-driven effort, people do not gravitate toward godliness, prayer, obedience to Scripture, faith, and delight in the Lord. We drift toward compromise and call it tolerance; we drift toward disobedience and call it freedom; we drift toward superstition and call it faith. We cherish the indiscipline of lost self-control and call it relaxation; we slouch toward prayerlessness and delude ourselves into thinking we have escaped legalism; we slide toward godlessness and convince ourselves we have been liberated."[9]

—D. A. CARSON

Today we've come full circle, landing in the exact same place we began when we first ventured into this study together. It's fitting and important that we land here again. At *obedience*. For not only is it the key that opens the door of communication with God, but it is also the stopper that keeps that door standing open wide, leading to the vast, abundant spaces of vibrant relationship with our heavenly Father. Obedience is not only the proactive posture we take to hear Him, but it is also the response we employ once He has spoken. In fact, no other response is appropriate.

Obedience. Always.

Obedience is not only the _____ _____ we take to hear Him, but it is also the _____ we employ once He has spoken.

Name one thing you've sensed God asking you to do since you've started this study that you have immediately and fully obeyed. What has been the outcome of your obedience?

Or, has God's Spirit convicted you to respond to His voice during the time you've been doing this study, and you *haven't* obeyed? Why not? What has been the result of your disobedience?

Obedience, as we all know (too well), remains hard to come by. Hard to motivate. But God, who is not surprised at our natural resistance to deny ourselves and follow Him, is invested in helping us get there. He wants us *"pure in heart"* so that we can see Him **(MATT. 5:8)**—and hear Him—and be led by Him into those places where we can be active participants in His plan for our times, plans that include you and me and a world of opportunity for us to serve Him together.

If we truly want to go there with Him, and if we want to go there in obedience, we will submit to His loving methods for showing us the way. And for this, we can learn another lesson from Habakkuk.

NO MATTER WHAT

Habakkuk has already proven to us his passion for hearing from God. We've even seen him climb a military tower, for Pete's sake, to assure he was in the best possible position for watching and listening. He was intentional—that's for sure.

But that's not all. He was braced for what God would tell Him. He didn't just want the good news; he wanted the bad and the ugly too. He wanted the truth. He wanted it all—whatever it cost and however hard it may have been to hear it.

Strong's *defines the word* reprove *in Habakkuk 2:1 as* "rebuke, correction, reproof, refutation, chastening."[10]

"I will stand on my guard post and station myself on the rampart; and I will keep watch to see what He will speak to me, and how I may reply when I am reproved."
HABAKKUK 2:1

Given the definition in the margin, what does Habakkuk's word choice imply about the type of response he expected from God?

Underline the portion of the verse that shows Habakkuk already thinking forward to what his response would be to God's Word.

When you anticipate this kind of sentiment from God's Spirit in regard to some area of your life, how does it affect your relationship with Him and your plans in regard to responding to Him?

Most scholars agree that the Hebrew word translated "reproved" in Habakkuk 2:1 is likely stronger than the more common word "complaint" that appears in many newer versions of Scripture. The prophet was anticipating a rebuke. He suspected God's reply would not be easy to digest. He wasn't fishing for a compliment. He believed some hard words were going to be said.

And yet, despite being fairly certain that he and his people were going to be called on the carpet for some serious offenses against God's character, he steeled himself on that watchtower, waiting, watching, prepared to obey what his God would tell him. He wouldn't be avoiding his Father. Even a rebuke, to him, was better than no word at all.

As a child, when I knew my dad or mom was going to chide me for a bad choice or behavior, I would avoid them at all costs. Suddenly I was far too busy doing those things I *loved* to do—you know, cleaning up my room or practicing the piano—too busy with my precious chores to be in their presence. I didn't really want to hear what they wanted to tell me, nor did I want the consequences that would extend from our conversation. So I steered clear. Kept a safe distance. Nobody the wiser.

I've done the same thing with God as well. I can't tell you how many times I've tiptoed into His presence or tried avoiding Him altogether because I was harboring secret worries that His response would be one I didn't want to hear. Whether I suspected He might want me to do something I didn't want to do, or might ask me *not* to do something I *did* want to do, I haven't always showed an eagerness to stay within earshot. Uncomfortable news is rarely the most welcome.

But when obedience is on the line—and when you've finally been through enough self-inflicted troublemaking at the hands of your own wants and agenda—the narrative changes. And like Habakkuk, you stand on that lookout post and say, *Bring it on, Lord, let's do this Your way. Give it to me straight now, because from here on out I want to walk a straight path with You.*

How do you usually respond to God's voice when He's saying something you don't want to hear? *Rank your responses from 1 to 4, 1 being the response you most frequently use, and 4 being the least frequent.*

_____ Ignore (act like I never heard it)

_____ Consider (weigh my other options and seek opinions)

_____ Obey (follow His directions regardless of how I feel)

_____ Keep praying (hope God will change His response)

Read the passages listed below, and draw a line that matches each one to God's response toward disobedience.

Jeremiah 6:16-19   Sent a famine of His Word

Amos 8:9-11   Refused to listen

Zechariah 7:12-13   Brought disaster to the people

Is there any way in which you've seen catastrophic outcomes like these in your own experiences or the life of another who refused to obey God?

I'll admit, many times when my commitment has been tested, I've failed miserably. I still acquiesce to certain areas of ego and pride, of fear and intimidation—far too easily and often—instead of stepping out in faith-filled obedience. God's Spirit has often given conviction that I have not been quick to follow, times when I've allowed my mind to rationalize me right out of obeying.

I'm grateful for His mercy and patience. I need it.

Lord Jesus, don't we all.

"When I kept silent about my sin, my body wasted away through my groaning all day long. For day and night Your hand was heavy upon me; my vitality was drained away as with the fever heat of summer."

PSALM 32:3-4

I'm learning that growth in this area will not happen by chance. It will only come from settling my own commitment to Him in advance of His direction so that I'll be less easily caught up in my own whims. I need a prearranged, internal posture of submission to God's Spirit, a "Yes, Lord" already falling from my lips, in order to prepare me for the actions necessary to honor Him on a daily basis.

See the verses from Psalm 32 in the margin. How did David, the writer of this psalm, say disobedience affected him?

Look up this psalm and read the remainder of it. What blessings and experiences of relief did David discover from taking an obedient, repentant approach?

The blessings of proactivity lead to continued intimacy with God, to the flow of His blessings and His favor in our lives. Oh, let me tell you, obedience is worth it.

Every single time.

DO YOU HEAR WHAT I HEAR?

Truth be told, I see you in Habakkuk. There aren't many believers who would spend a whole month and a half of their lives dedicated to the task of exploring this subject—*Discerning the Voice of God.* The fact that you've followed through on it is commendable, proof of how seriously you take this aspect of your relationship with Him, how you hunger to hear Him.

So I'm assuming you want the same thing I do. I believe you want to ensure that this door of communication between you and God remains flung open, the lines of communication cleared of any impediment that might inhibit the kind of relationship with Him that you were created to experience. Yet true blessing is not only found in *hearing* God's voice but in *heeding* it. When you obey, no matter how unusual or unwanted His instructions may be, you create a solid foundation on which He can display His supernatural activity in your life.

He will honor you for climbing up this watchtower, my friend.

THE FIFTH DAY

I'm going to miss this. Writing to you. Sharing with you.

But one thing that will really keep me encouraged as we part ways for now is knowing that while I'm out here continuing to learn and grow in this discipline of hearing God's voice, you'll be out there as well, with your heart and Bible open, with your will surrendered and toggled toward obedience—listening.

So would you mind bearing with me one last moment while we practice some listening tips together?

I think we all know the difference between passive and aggressive listening. Passive listening is when someone's talking, you hear them, you see their lips moving, but you're not really digesting or internalizing what they're saying. Hearing God, of course, doesn't happen best this way—through distracted, disinterested listening. Certainly He can cause His voice, the Spirit's conviction, or even a deep-seated impression to hit us full force if that's what He so chooses, no matter how loud the surroundings. But to best prime our spiritual ears to hear Him, we can't always be doing fifteen things at once. If you and I think we can spend night after night watching television, robotically surfing the Internet, keeping our mental real estate chock-full of other interests, our souls burdened with earthly affairs—and still hear God clearly, by passively listening for Him—we're not living in reality. Posturing ourselves to hear from the Lord means punctuating our prayer time with the antiquated art of silence, turning our attention inward to detect the stirring of God's Spirit, looking intently at the Word, and loving what it says more than we love what everyone and everything else around us is saying.

Which activities most often rob you of opportunities to be still before God?

What types of emotional responses does the thought of stillness and solitude strike in you?

○ Unsettledness
○ Anxiety
○ Boredom
○ Calm
○ Other _____ _____ _____

In case you find what I'm suggesting to be completely unrealistic in your current everyday dynamic and season of life, hear me—you can still *aggressively listen* for God's voice, even amid the busy, unavoidable, important demands of your ongoing routine. We don't need to be monks or nuns to be able to receive divine direction.

I've been learning to look and listen for Him while doing all sorts of mundane tasks. I frequently ask Him to heighten my spiritual senses so I can detect Him whenever He's moving and speaking. In conversation with a stranger, when playing outside with my boys, when washing a load of dirty dishes, when planning for an event, *God is there*. If I'm asking Him to reveal Himself, He will do it—as He chooses—through little whispers, confirmations, divine delays, and heavenly echoes that corroborate with what He's already been saying to me through His Word and His Spirit.

Make a list of everyday tasks you'll be doing today or tomorrow. How can you turn them into opportunities to aggressively listen for God to speak? *(Use the following chart, or you might need a separate piece of paper for this exercise.)*

TASK	HOW I CAN AGGRESSIVELY LISTEN

What you've read in your quiet time or heard from your pastor at church the previous Sunday is not disconnected from the happenings of a regular morning, afternoon, or evening. If you'll consider Him throughout the day, even when it's a busy one, He'll weave it all together so you can know His will and ways—as long as you're actively listening.

I love knowing we'll be doing that together—today, tomorrow—till we see Him face-to-face, with nothing ever again coming between us and His presence, with nothing ever again coming between us and, yes, the sound of—

His voice.

THE RIGHT ATMOSPHERE

by Dr. Tony Evans

Some time ago, a foul smell began permeating our education center—the largest, most expensive building on our church campus. We spent thousands of dollars trying to identify and correct the problem, all to no avail. As a result, people avoided going inside the building because the atmosphere was not conducive for usefulness.

One day, a member of our janitorial staff noticed the ceiling fans in the restrooms were turning the wrong way. Instead of lifting the smell up and out, they were pushing the smell down and back inside. A simple reversal of direction changed everything.

Atmosphere matters. You're unlikely to eat in an unsanitary restaurant no matter how good the food tastes. If you have bad customer service at a retail store, you'll drive out of your way to shop somewhere else next time. All because atmosphere matters.

The same is true when it comes to hearing God's voice. The Spirit must feel welcome in the lives of those who desire to have fellowship with Him. This is why Paul admonishes us to let Christ *"dwell"* in our hearts **(EPH. 3:17)**—to be at home there. It's why he exhorts believers to *"pray without ceasing"* **(1 THESS. 5:17)** and stay in a constant atmospheric state of communicating with God about every aspect of our lives. It's why Jesus says He *"stand[s] at the door and knock[s]"* **(REV. 3:20)**, waiting for us to open to Him so we can have an intimate relationship.

God will not communicate in an atmosphere of conflict, which is why the prayers of husbands are not heard when men are at odds with their wives (1 Pet. 3:7), and why a couple can expect to hear His voice when they are unified (1 Cor. 7:5). Atmosphere matters.

He will not communicate in an atmosphere of evil and unrighteousness, since sin blocks fellowship. As Isaiah wrote, *"Behold, the* LORD's *hand is not so short that it cannot save; nor is His ear so dull that it cannot hear. But your iniquities have made a separation between you and your God, and your sins have hidden His face from you so that He does not hear"* **(ISA. 59:1-2)**. Only when we are passionately pursuing a relationship with Him, repenting of our sins, promoting unity and not disunity—only then do we create an atmosphere conducive for God to manifest His will to us in a personal way.

The question is simply this: *How badly do you want it?* When you make hearing His voice the primary pursuit of your life, you can expect to hear Him more clearly than ever before.

Build God a runway on which His glory and kingdom can land, and you will see Him as you've never seen Him before. You will hear Him as you've never heard him before. You will know Him and be known by Him as never before. Remember, atmosphere matters.

Speak, Lord

#DISCERNINGTHEVOICE

WEEK SEVEN

*Video sessions available for purchase at
www.LifeWay.com/DiscerningTheVoiceOfGod.*

LEADER GUIDE

SESSION ONE

DISCUSSION STARTER: After meeting others in the group, encourage women to discuss what drew them to participate in this *Discerning the Voice of God* study. Ask the women in the group: What first comes to mind when they think of hearing from God? Does hearing from God come easily or has it been a struggle? Talk through expectations for the study.

READ JOHN 5:30 AND DISCUSS Jesus' submission to God the Father's will in all that He did. With Jesus as our model, what might submission to the Father's will look like in our everyday lives? Does this come easily to most of us? Why or why not?

WATCH THE WEEK ONE VIDEO.

- What resonated most with you from the video teaching?

- How do you struggle with stillness and prayer? What can you do to intentionally practice stillness?

- Have you ever been reluctant to obey something you felt God was telling you to do because you didn't think God would "work" in that way? If you feel comfortable, please share that story with the group.

CLOSE WITH PRAYER.

SESSION TWO

DISCUSSION STARTER: Review the story of Abraham and Isaac in Genesis 22:2-3. Ask women to share what comes to mind when they hear the word *obedience*. Has their understanding of that term changed since they were children? Ask women to share (as much as they are comfortable) the areas in which they sense God asking

them to make some changes as they walk forward in obedience to Him **(P. 27)**. Talk through counting the cost—the tension between loss and reward, doubt and faith.

READ JOHN 16:5-15 AND DISCUSS the God-given roles of the Holy Spirit in our lives. Ask women what preconceived notions about the Holy Spirit they bring to the table.

WATCH THE WEEK TWO VIDEO.

- What, if anything, in the video teaching challenged the way you currently view the Holy Spirit and His work in your life? How have you seen Him work in your life up to this point? Are you willing to adjust your preferences and decisions as the Holy Spirit leads? Reference the "Red light, Yellow Light, Green Light" illustration and its usefulness in understanding the Holy Spirit's guidance.

- Discuss the Body/Soul/Spirit diagram **(P. 48)** that Priscilla describes in the video teaching. Ask women to speak about a time God allowed them to see His sanctification process in their lives—perhaps a time where their desires, actions, or thoughts shifted in a more "Godward" direction.

ASK FOR A VOLUNTEER TO CLOSE YOUR TIME IN PRAYER.

SESSION THREE

DISCUSSION STARTER: Briefly discuss the "Five Ms of Correctly Hearing God" **(P. 55)**. Which of these was particularly encouraging/challenging? Does the idea of "practicing" to discern God's voice make sense and come naturally or why might it seem a bit strange at first?

READ JOHN 10:27-30 AND DISCUSS God's role as our shepherd. Take a moment to focus on verse 27, *"My sheep hear My voice, and I know them, and they follow Me..."* talking through God's intentionality to speak in a way that His children can hear.

WATCH THE WEEK THREE VIDEO.

- Ask women to share a story of a time they clearly heard God's direction. Or, perhaps, a time when God asked them to wait.

- Discuss Priscilla's quote "Waiting on God means being obedient and fully engaged in what He has currently given you to do until your Guide tells you to take the next turn." Is there an area that you've been asking God to work in and He seems to be moving more slowly than you like? If we applied this quote to our situations, how would that inform our daily walks and attitudes about our current circumstances?

AS A GROUP, PRAY SPECIFICALLY FOR THINGS IN YOUR LIVES THAT YOU'RE SEEKING THE LORD ABOUT.

SESSION FOUR

DISCUSSION STARTER: Focusing on God's Word can sometimes seem like a daunting task, especially when it's a new practice. Discuss the practice of continually thinking over God's Word in Bible study and throughout the day. Then, reference your priorities list **(P. 90).** Ask women what they would need to do to make studying and praying God's Word a priority. Make sure to talk about the practice of dwelling on God's Word throughout the day, "as they go." They can think on God's Word while folding laundry, driving, grocery shopping, or running on the treadmill.

READ JOHN 8:1-11 AND DISCUSS the difference between Jesus' reaction and the reaction of the Scribes and Pharisees to the woman caught in adultery. When discerning the voice of God, we'll need to learn to discern the voice of others—so we can disregard their speech in favor of God's instructions. In this passage, how do we see God's voice of conviction versus the Pharisees' voices of condemnation?

WATCH THE WEEK FOUR VIDEO.

- In times of seeking God's will on particular issues, why do we often get stressed and quickly frustrated? Are our actions and attitudes showing us that we believe it's "up to us" to hear what God is saying? What's the truth?

- In searching for God's instruction, have you found yourself losing sight of God Himself in favor of the things He may give? Why is that such a common temptation? Discuss how you might refocus your efforts to get to know God for Himself and not for the blessings or instruction He could give you.

PRAY FOR EACH INDIVIDUAL WOMAN IN YOUR GROUP. ASK GOD TO TEACH YOU MORE ABOUT HIS HEART AND CHARACTER.

SESSION FIVE

DISCUSSION STARTER: In last week's study, we talked about the difference between encouragement, conviction, and condemnation. God brings us encouragement and conviction, while the enemy brings condemnation. As you studied these differences, have you been able to more readily identify God's encouragement (versus the enemy's condemnation or discouragement) in your thought life? If you're comfortable, share an example with the group. Along the same lines, what do you think about measuring your thoughts and actions against Scripture? What would it look like to make that a more regular practice in your life?

READ EPHESIANS 2:10. God says we are His workmanship. How does the idea of God's guiding hand in crafting us to look more like Himself inform the way that you understand discerning His voice? Does His commitment to sanctify you bring you comfort or stress? Explain.

WATCH THE WEEK FIVE VIDEO.

- In difficult circumstances, why does it take an intentional effort to shift our focus from our surroundings? When you are in a desert season, do you run *to* God or run *from* God? Why do you think you respond in that way?

- Is it easy for you to believe that God's plans for your life—even if they require a detour or delay—are truly the best for you? What might keep you from trusting Him and waiting for Him to do the best?

CLOSE IN PRAYER.

SESSION SIX

DISCUSSION STARTER: Take a moment to talk through several of the biblical examples that you explored this week (P. 144). Make sure to raise the question of God's timing and the way He orchestrated the circumstances in their lives. What do these stories tell you about God's character?

READ HABAKKUK 1:5. (Feel free to read the surrounding verses in the passage, beginning at Hab. 1:1, for more context.) Discuss God's power and ability to move in astonishing ways—He often works imperceptibly both on our behalves and to bring glory to His own name. Take a moment in your group to brainstorm some of the reasons that we struggle to expect great things from God. What's a practical way that we could help change those expectations in our hearts and minds?

WATCH THE WEEK SIX VIDEO.

- As a follower of Christ, what does it mean to you to be a part of the family of God? Have you really allowed that to become part of your identity and change your everyday life? If that's a struggle for you, what holds you back? Do you think owning your identity might make a difference in your heart and mind?

- Priscilla says, "If the enemy cannot destroy you, he will just try to distract you." How has technology been a distraction in your life, pulling you away from more important priorities? What kinds of strategies can you implement for yourself and your family members to incorporate healthy boundaries when it comes to social media and technological devices?

ASK A GROUP MEMBER TO PRAY FOR YOUR LAST WEEK OF STUDY.

SESSION SEVEN

DISCUSSION STARTER: Think back to our study of Habakkuk and reference the things that God promised Habakkuk in chapter 2, verse 3. Which of these promises brings you the most encouragement? Which promise was most challenging to you in your time of study? If you're seeking the Lord on a particular issue, which of these promises do you most struggle to believe in that specific circumstance?

READ HABAKKUK 2:1 AND DISCUSS Habakkuk's approach to waiting on the Lord and his eagerness to be corrected by the Lord. Do we share those same characteristics in approaching God? Why or why not?

WATCH THE WEEK SEVEN VIDEO.

- Lead women in a prayer time. Ask God for revival, not only the hearts of the women in your group, but also in the families, churches, and communities represented.

- As you finish your study time together, take a moment to reflect back on specific truths from this study that have proven particularly impactful in this season of life. Ask the women to recount ways they've heard from God and seen Him move as you review each week of the study. Praise Him for His goodness and for the women you've been able to walk this journey

with. Challenge women to use the end of this study as a jumping off point for a more intimate relationship with God. This is just the beginning of the rest of their lives in knowing God more intimately and discerning His leading more clearly.

ENDNOTES

WEEK ONE

1. Lewis Sperry Chafer, *He That is Spiritual: A Classic Study of the Biblical Doctrine of Spirituality* (Grand Rapids: Zondervan, 1967), 92.

2. Roger Staubach as quoted in Jay Stewart, *The Ultimate Road Trip: 12 Journeys that Shape Your Future* (Shippensburg, PA: Destiny Image Publishers, Inc., 2010).

3. Alfred J. Hoerth, *Archaeology and the Old Testament* (Grand Rapids: Baker Academic, 1998), 104.

4. John Baillie, *A Diary of Private Prayer* (New York: Scribner, 1949).

5. James Strong, *Strong's Exhaustive Concordance of the Bible*, accessed on April 20, 2017, *Blue Letter Bible* available online via *blueletterbible.org/lang/lexicon/lexicon. cfm?Strongs=G1718&t=KJV.*

WEEK TWO

1. Stephen F. Olford and David L. Olford, *Anointed Expository Preaching* (Nashville: B & H, 1998), 29-30.

2. Charles R. Swindoll, "How Do I Know God's Will?" Insight for Today from Chuck Swindoll, *Christianity.com*, June 30, 2014, accessed on May 16, 2017, available online via *christianity. com/print/11714665/.*

3. Horatius Bonar as quoted in Peter Lord, *Hearing God* (Bloomington, MN: Chosen Books, 1988), 27.

WEEK THREE

1. Definition of "Guide," *Blue Letter Bible*, accessed on June 5, 2017, available online via *blueletterbible.org/lang/lexicon/lexicon. cfm?Strongs=G3594&t=KJV.*

2. F. B. Meyer, *The Secret of Guidance* (Chicago: Moody Publishers, 1997), 10.

3. Ibid, 13.

4. Definition of "Treasured," *Blue Letter Bible*, accessed on June 16, 2017, available online

via *blueletterbible.org/lang/lexicon/lexicon. cfm?t=esv&strongs=g4933.*

WEEK FOUR

1. A. W. Tozer, *Man: The Dwelling Place of God* (Camp Hill, PA: WingSpread Publishers, 1966) via *mywsb.com* accessed on June 1, 2017.

2. Brother Lawrence, *The Practice of the Presence of God and Spiritual Maxims* (Incense House Publishing, 2013), 45.

3. W. F. Arndt, F. W. Danker, F. W. Gingrich, *A Greek-English Lexicon of the New Testament and Other Early Christian Literature*, Third Edition (Chicago: The University of Chicago Press, 2000), 258.

4. Andreas J. Köstenberger, *John: Baker Exegetical Commentary on the New Testament* (Grand Rapids, MI: Baker Academic, 2004), 474.

5. Jan Johnson, *When the Soul Listens* (Colorado Springs: NavPress, 1999), 156.

6. Bob Sorge, *Secrets of the Secret Place* (Grandview, MO: Oasis House, 2001), 57-58.

7. Definition of "Rule," *Blue Letter Bible*, accessed on June 5, 2017, available online via *blueletterbible.org/lang/lexicon/lexicon. cfm?Strongs=G1018&t=KJV.*

WEEK FIVE

1. C. S. Lewis, *The Problem of Pain* (New York: HarperCollins, 1996), 92.

2. Bruce Wilkinson, *Secrets of the Vine* (Colorado Springs: Multnomah Books, 2001).

3. Quoted in R. T. Kendall, *The Sensitivity of the Spirit* (Lake Mary, FL: Charisma House, 2002), 98-99.

4. "The Official Website of Arthur Blessitt" accessed on June 5, 2017, available online via *blessitt.com.*

5. "Listed in the New Guinness World Records 2015, Page 155" *Official Website of Arthur*

Blessitt, accessed on June 5, 2017, available online via *blessitt.com/guinness-world-records/*.

6. "Longest Ongoing Pilgrimage" *Guinness World Records* accessed on June 5, 2017, available online via *guinnessworldrecords.com/world-records/longest-ongoing-pilgrimage*.

7. Ibid, Kendall.

8. Henry T. Blackaby and Richard Blackaby, *Hearing God's Voice* (Nashville: B & H, 2002), 46.

9. Ibid, Tozer, *Man: the Dwelling Place of God*.

10. Elisabeth Elliot, *God's Guidance: A Slow and Certain Light* (Ada, MI: Revell, 1997), 92.

11. Ibid, Johnson, 129.

12. Ibid, Blackaby and Blackaby, 202.

13. Matt Crocker, Joel Houston, and Salomon Lightelm, *Oceans (Where Feet May Fail)*. Brentwood, TN: Sparrow Records, 2013.

14. Ibid, Johnson, 112.

15. Peter Lord, *Hearing God* (Bloomington, MN: Chosen Books, 1988), 190.

WEEK SIX

1. Ibid, Sorge, 11.

2. A. W. Tozer, *The Root of the Righteous* (Chicago: Moody, 2015), 27-28.

3. Ibid, Kendall.

4. John Powell as quoted in Joyce Huggett, *Listening to God, 30th Anniversary Edition* (London: Hodder & Stoughton Ltd., 2016).

5. Definition of "Amad," *Bible Study Tools*, accessed on June 14, 2017, available online via *biblestudytools.com/lexicons/hebrew/nas/amad.html*.

6. Definition of "Yatsab," *Bible Study Tools*, accessed on June 14, 2017, available online via *biblestudytools.com/lexicons/hebrew/nas/yatsab.html*.-

7. Ibid, Sorge, 11.

8. Ibid, Huggett.

9. D. A. Carson, *For the Love of God, Volume Two* (Wheaton: Crossway, 1999).

10. Definition of "Reprove," *Blue Letter Bible*, accessed on June 5, 2017, available online via *blueletterbible.org/lang/lexicon/lexicon.cfm?Strongs=H8433&t=KJV*.

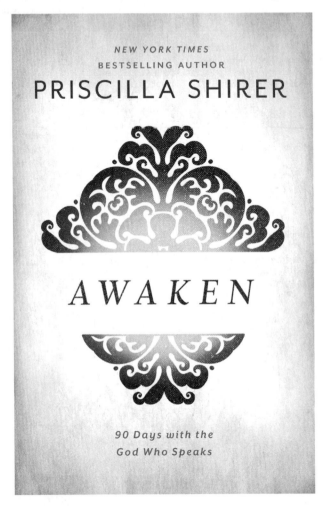

Other Studies by Priscilla

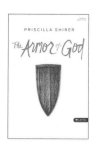

THE ARMOR OF GOD
7 sessions

The enemy always fails miserably when he meets a woman dressed for the occasion. Develop your own personalized strategy to secure victory against the enemy.

Bible Study Book 005727075 **$12.99**
Leader Kit 005727076 **$149.99**

LifeWay.com/ArmorOfGod

BREATHE: MAKING ROOM FOR SABBATH
5 sessions

If you are weary, worn out, and exhausted, the concept of Sabbath will change your life. Challenge yourself to break your devotion to busyness, and gain back your peace from Him alone.

Study Journal 005644896 **$9.99**
Leader Kit 005656144 **$99.99**

LifeWay.com/Breathe

ONE IN A MILLION: JOURNEY TO YOUR PROMISED LAND
7 sessions

Only two out of two million Israelites crossed over into the promised land. Discover direction for your spiritual life, and expect to see God move in miraculous ways.

Bible Study Book 005169734 **$12.99**
Leader Kit 005169733 **$149.99**

LifeWay.com/OneInAMillion

GIDEON: YOUR WEAKNESS. GOD'S STRENGTH.
7 sessions

Learn to recognize your weakness as the key God gives you to unlock the full experience of His strength in your life.

Bible Study Book 005538485 **$12.99**
Leader Kit 005538484 **$149.99**

LifeWay.com/Gideon

JONAH: NAVIGATING A LIFE INTERRUPTED
7 sessions

Redefine life's many interruptions as God's invitation to do something greater than we could ever imagine.

Bible Study Book 005264295 **$12.99**
Leader Kit 005189429 **$149.99**

LifeWay.com/LifeInterrupted

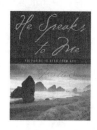

HE SPEAKS TO ME: PREPARING TO HEAR FROM GOD
7 sessions

Study the story of how God spoke to the boy Samuel, how he responded, and discover how God speaks to believers—and you—today.

Bible Study Book 001269686 **$12.99**
Leader Kit 001269687 **$149.99**

LifeWay.com/HeSpeaksToMe

DEVOTIONS WITH PRISCILLA AUDIO CD

Take this collection of 12 devotional teaching segments on the go, with each about 10 minutes long, taken from Priscilla's popular Bible studies.

Audio CD Set 005271627 **$5.00**

LifeWay | Women

LifeWay.com/PriscillaShirer
800.458.2772 | LifeWay Christian Stores

Pricing and availability subject to change without notice.